Character Dance

Character Dance

Andrei Lopoukov, Alexander Shirayev
and Alexander Bocharov

Translated by Joan Lawson

Dance Books

This book was first published in Russian in 1939 in honour of
the 200th anniversary of the founding of the School in Rossi Street
now The Choreographic Academy of Dance named Vaganova, Leningrad.

This translation first published in 1986 by Dance Books Ltd.

© 1986 Joan Lawson.

British Library Cataloguing in Publication Data

Lopoukhov, Andrei
   Character dance.
   1. Ballet
   I. Title   II. Shirayev, Alexander
   III. Bocharov, Alexander
   792.8'2   GV1788

ISBN 0-903102-90-0

Contents

Introduction	7
Exercises at the barre	10
Introduction to studies in character dance	52
Studies in character dance:	
1. Russian dance	56
2. Hungarian dance	80
3. Polish dance	93
4. Gipsy dance	101
5. Spanish dance	108

Introduction

This book was published in 1939 and had been compiled to celebrate the two hundredth anniversary of the founding of what is now the Leningrad Choreographic Academy named Vaganova. The three authors, Shirayev, Lopoukov and Bocharov, had all been brilliant character dancers with the Marinsky, Diaghilev and other companies before becoming teachers and/or choreographers at the school and with the Kirov Ballet. Because they were then establishing a five-year Course in Character Dance as part of the whole syllabus at the school they worked in collaboration with Yuri Ossipovitch Slonimsky, the Soviet critic, historian and librettist. His methods of work ensured that their wide ranging knowledge would be given as concise a form as possible.

I have personally experienced Slonimsky's generosity, sympathy and above all clarity of thought when working in any field of dance. His introduction, in the original Russian edition of this book, to the work of these authors is masterly for he writes of how the simple folk dances of many European peoples gradually evolved to become on the one hand the court and social dances of the 16th, 17th, 18th and 19th centuries and on the other the classical and character dances of the theatre. He brings to light many historical details of the work of such choreographers as Didelot, Bournonville, Saint-Léon and Fokine and their use of folk dance. He asserts that whatever character dance be performed on stage, it must communicate the particular style, mood, quality of movement and musical features of its place of origin. However it can never be an exact replica of the real thing, because even today in remote areas of the world, genuine folk dance is still a form of ritual in which certain, if not all, able-bodied persons of a particular community have a part to play if the ritual is to achieve the desired result. Such dances are not meant for an audience. The purpose is known to the participants only. On the other hand character dance is directly aimed to an audience. Its purposes are different. It is often used to give local colour to the setting of the scene and unfolding of the plot as in *Petrushka* or *The Three Cornered Hat*. It can add to the spectacle as in *Swan Lake* or *The Nutcracker*.

Ever since Didelot, Bournonville, Saint-Léon, Fokine and others began to produce ballets whose plots were laid in one particular country, choreographers have added to those first attempts to codify all the elements of those peoples whose dancing seems to have attracted most attention in the Western world, namely Italy, Scotland, Hungary, Poland, Spain, Russia and the Ukraine. This is certainly the case when studying 19th century ballets. Since the Russian Revolution of 1917 Soviet experts have drawn attention to the dances of Georgia, Bashkiria, Uzbekistan and other republics whose dances now appear in Soviet ballets. But it is not only in the U.S.S.R. that choreographers have studied and utilised the dances of their own countries. This is particularly the case with the Balkan countries and Slonimsky does mention the enormous work being done in this field even though no sections of this book are devoted to those particular features. It is an enormous undertaking as it contains some four hundred exercises and studies. As some of these would only be of value to Soviet dancers and make the work too large to handle, I have thought it best to translate only those items valuable to Western dancers whose work in the classical ballet theatre will require a knowledge of Russian, Polish, Hungarian, Spanish and Gipsy character dance, as well as a brief study on running, which is possibly the best view of all. It demonstrates how many different ways a dancer can run on the stage to give characterisation to this simple movement.

The three authors have been very careful to time each exercise to the beats of the music. They also add some thoughts on how to compose studies for one or another country. They are included in the text. But from my own experience of character classes with many Soviet teachers, the following may also be of use when creating suitable *enchainements* for practice.

Russian Dance.
If it is to be a group dance then it is typical to work in circles which break into undulating lines and reform. One step should be repeated at least 4, but usually at least 8 times before changing to another. However when using *Drumming* it is essential to perform some kind of *Break* or stop every 8 bars.

If on the other hand a solo is intended it should be as brief as 16 bars and never more than 32 and contain four steps at the most and two if the solo is intended to make a sensation.

Polish Dance.
Is somewhat similar to Russian in the way the *enchainements* are built, but attention must be paid to the patterning of the figures in all Mazurkas and Krakoviaks which should be danced by four, eight or sixteen couples who change partners from time to time as they cross and re-cross the set, but always return to their own. Each *enchainement* must finish with a *Break* and a very clear change of step must be seen at the opening of the next phrase.

Hungarian and Gipsy Dance.
Each *enchainement* should contain a variety of steps even though it must finish with a break at the end of each musical phrase. It is also usual to

repeat an *enchainement* – no matter how short or long – no more than twice, unlike the Polish when one *enchainement* is repeated throughout a figure being danced by each couple in turn.

Gipsy dance must always appear to be unexpected thus steps change more rapidly from one into the other and it is important that when dancing in couples the one and then the other pauses to admire the partner's efforts. Thus poses have to be struck and held.

Spanish Dance.
This is so varied that little guidance is given as to how *enchainements* should be formed. Nevertheless many of the traditional forms of advancing and retiring in couples are known and the one item stressed is the need for the couple to keep in eye contact throughout.

Joan Lawson.

POSITIONS OF THE FEET

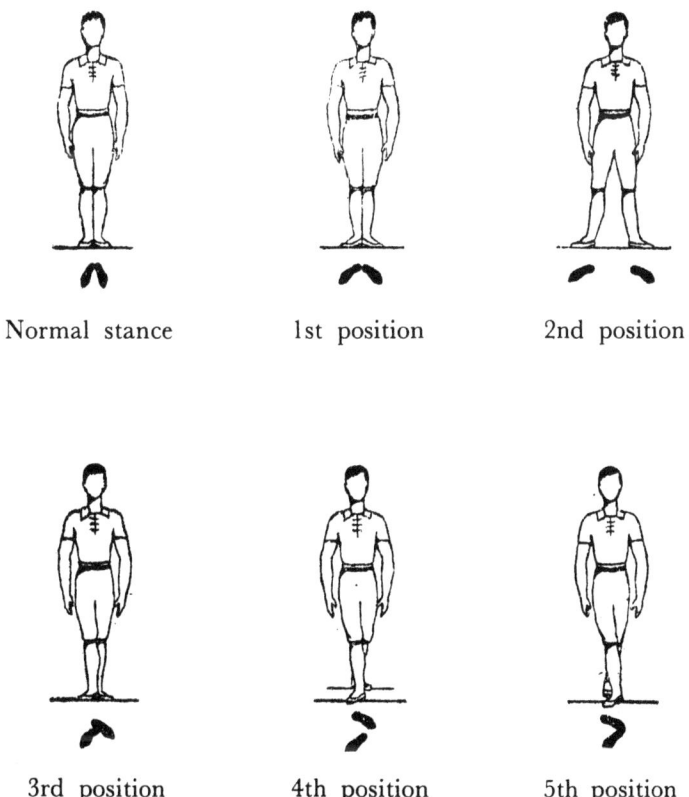

Exercises at the Barre

A literal translation into words of these essential character exercises is not fully possible. Oral instruction can only supply the minute details about the stretching of the foot, accent and phrasing; however the basic principles of stance, turn-out and co-ordination of body and arms – so much a part of classical dance – must be maintained.

1. PLIES.
No. 1. Simple.
Time signature 4/4. Commence in 1st position.
1.2. With R hand on hip, bend knees slightly (quarter *plié*) and stretch.
3.4. Repeat quarter *plié*.
5.6.7. Full *plié* and stretch.
8. Raise R arm to 3rd, changing the body into slight *épaulment éffacé* at the same time lightly stamping R foot into 3rd *derrière*.
1–7. Repeat above in 3rd *derrière* lowering R hand to hip on 1st quarter *plié*.
8. Stamp R foot into 1st position raising R arm to 3rd and bring body *de face*.
1–8. Repeat whole, on 8th beat stamping R foot in 3rd *devant* at the same time bringing the body *croisé* and raising arm to 3rd.
1–8. Repeat as above and on 8th beat finish with stamp in 1st bringing body *de face*.

No. 2. Complex.
Time signature 4/4.
Introduction 4 beats (1 bar). Commence in 1st position, hands at side of body.

1. Place L hand on barre.
2. Open R arm to low 2nd, moving it through 1st.
3. Place R hand on R hip.
4. Pause.

1st bar.
1. *Demi-plié.*
2. Stretch knees.
3. *Demi-plié..* raising R arm to 1st.
4. Stretch knees.

2nd bar.
1–2. Full *plié* bending body slightly to left and lowering R arm just in front of L knee.
3. Stretch knees opening R arm to low 2nd, palm upwards and bending slightly backwards to right.
4. Straighten body and head, holding R arm in 2nd.

3rd bar.
Repeat 2nd bar.

4th. bar.
1. *Demi-plié* placing R hand on hip.
2. Stretch knees.
3. Quarter *plié* rising on *demi-pointes* and turning knees inwards immediately straighten them and turn feet outwards and rest on heels.
4. Place toes on floor in small 2nd position.

Bars 5–7.
Repeat bars 1–3 in 2nd position.

Bar 8.
1. *Demi-plié.*
2. Stretch knees.
3. Quarter *plié* turning toes inwards so that they all but touch.
and. Rise on *demi-pointes* turning legs outwards so that R foot comes in front of L.
4. Lower heels in 5th position, stretching knees.

Bars 9–11.
Repeat bars 1–3 in 5th position. R foot *devant.*

Bar 12.
1. *Demi-plié.*
2. Straighten knees.
3. Quarter *plié* rising on *demi-pointes* turning knees inwards.
and. Still on *demi-pointes* turning knees outwards (still bent), twist R foot behind L.
4. Lower heels, R foot now in 5th *derrière.*

Bars 13–15.
Repeat bars 1–3 in 5th, R foot *derrière*.

Bar 16.
1. *Demi-plié*.
2. Stretch knees.
3. Quarter *plié* rising on *demi-pointes* turning legs inwards.
and. Still on *demi-pointes* turn legs outwards bringing R foot in front of L.
4. Lower heels and stretch knees in 5th position.
Repeat whole on other side.
N.B. Further *plié* exercises are to be found in Studies for Russian dance and other squatting steps.

2. CHARACTER BATTEMENTS TENDUS.

The connection between the classical and character versions of these *battements tendus* lies in their different qualities. If the first variant seems only a slightly more accented version than that performed in a classical class, then the following versions will gradually reveal how the quality of the movement must differ. The sixth version has no connection with classical dance.

No. 1. (A first exercise.)
Time signature 2/4. Commence in 3rd position. R foot *devant*, R hand on hip.
anacrusis.* Open R *pointe tendue 4th devant*.
1. Draw R foot back into 3rd with light stamp simultaneously lifting L heel and bending L knee, but leaving L toe on floor.
2. Lower L heel immediately sliding R leg out sideways *pointe tendue*.
1–2. Repeat above bringing R foot back to 3rd before opening it to *pointe tendue derrière* (i.e. perform exercise *en croix*).

Anacrusis. An unstressed note or group of notes at the beginning of a musical phrase, or, in the usual language of the dancing class "AND", a warning to be ready. If followed by some direction it means the step starts before the first beat of the bar. If not, it warns the dancer to be ready to start on the first beat. This difference is particularly important in Slav dance.

EXERCISES AT THE BARRE

The principles of classical dance must be maintained except when the feet are joined in 3rd. At this point the supporting knee is bent and the heel of the supporting foot raised.

Repeat exercises no more than 4 times *en croix* with each leg.

No. 2.
Time signature 2/4. Commence in 3rd position, R foot *devant*, R hand on hip. anacrusis. Raise R heel and turn R foot inwards keeping leg as straight as possible, but not tense. R toes should rest on *demi-pointes* and should be parallel to L heel.
1. Turn R leg outwards and draw foot back to 3rd.
and. Repeat movement as in anacrusis.
2. Repeat 1, but bend both knees in small *demi-plié*.
and. repeat movement of anacrusis.

This exercise, because of its simplicity, must be given early, and be repeated 16 times with each foot.

The mistakes made are those of twisting the hips with the turn of the foot. The movement must come directly from the working hip-joint, the body being motionless. The exercise must develop the turn-out of the working leg and should follow No. 1.

No. 3.

Time signature 2/4. Commence in 3rd, R foot *devant*, R hand on hip, knees slightly bent.
anacrusis. Bend L knee and Raise L heel from floor.
1. Stamp L heel simultaneously stretching R leg *pointe tendue devant*.
and. Keeping R leg stretched, reverse R foot placing heel on floor.
2. Repeat stamp on L heel and again reverse R foot to *pointe tendue*.
and. Draw R foot back to 3rd with light stamp.

The whole exercise must be repeated *en croix* from 8–16 times with each foot during 1st year of training and care must be taken to ensure the slight and easy bending of the supporting leg.

This movement is very typical of character work with its contrast between the easy bending of the knees and feet together with the sharp but light stamp to bring the foot back to its proper position. The spine must be kept very erect, weight held firmly over the supporting leg at all times, whether the knee is bent or stretched. The shoulders, in particular, must be held firmly and not rock with the feet. The exercise aims to strengthen the calf, ankle and thigh muscles.

No. 4.

Time signature 2/4. Commence 3rd position, R foot *devant*, R hand on hip.
1. Stretch R to *pointe tendue devant*.
and. With a swift movement of the foot, brush R heel on floor and raise R leg slightly upwards, toe turned up.
2. Replace R toe on floor.
and. Return R foot to 3rd position.

The knees must be held straight throughout this exercise, which should not be introduced too early.

This exercise should also be practised with a *demi-plié* before the working foot returns to 3rd. It is usually performed eight times without and then eight times with the *demi-plié*.

The time signature should also be changed to 3/4 in which case the turn from toe to heel and toe is quicker.

Another way of completing this *battement* is not to return the foot to 3rd, but to stamp the whole foot on the floor in the open position. It is essential to make an absolutely clear and sharp bend from the toe to the heel and back. Students must not be allowed to grip their toes, otherwise they cramp the movement of the ankle.

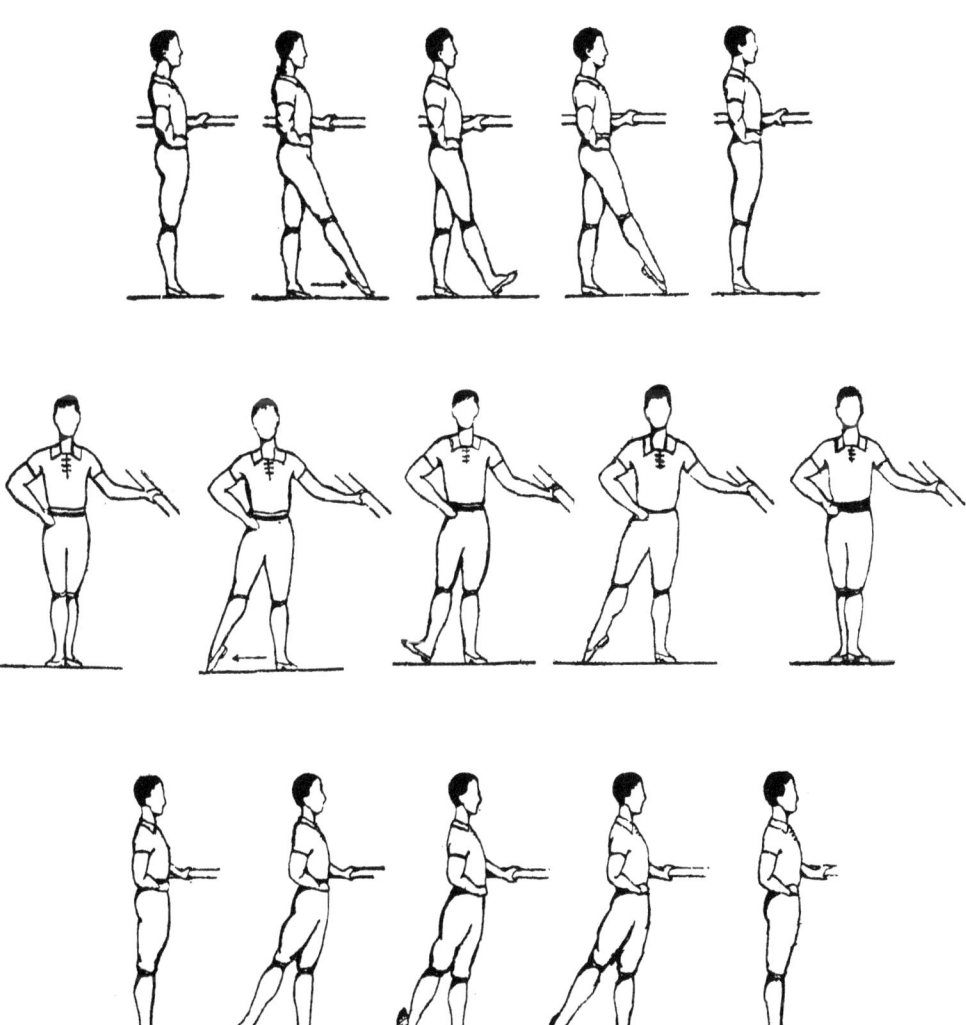

No. 5.

This contains no elements of classical dance and does not use the fully stretched *pointe tendue*. Instead by turning the leg *en dedans* the student achieves quite the opposite result and stretches the back of the leg. This exercise is best danced together with No. 3.

Time signature 2/4. Commence in 3rd, R foot *devant*, R hand on hip.
anacrusis. Bend L knee, raising L heel from floor.

Bar 1.
1. Strike L heel on floor raising R foot to L ankle.
and. Brush R foot out sideways to rest heel on floor, toe upwards and lifting L heel.
2. Strike L heel on floor, turning R leg inwards and raising it slightly bent.
and. Lightly beat R toe, leg turned-in, beating it parallel to L foot and raising L heel.

Bar 2.
1. Repeat striking L heel on floor but raise R leg turning it outwards with toe up.
and. Strike R heel on floor, raising L heel as before.
2. Strike L heel on floor, bending R knee and resting foot behind L ankle.
and. Stamp R foot behind L in 3rd.
This final stamp can be performed with a straight or bent knee.
Repeat 8–16 times with each foot.

The importance of this exercise is to prepare for the easy turning inwards and outwards of the working leg in such movements as *pas tortillés*.

The basic mistake in this exercise is the tendency to twist waist and shoulders with the turning in and out of the working foot. The student must keep hips and shoulders square and held firmly. The supporting leg must be held directly under the body and in the same place on the floor. The exercise should enter the vocabulary later and should be combined with No. 3.

No. 6. (This is introduced only when the previous exercises have been mastered.)
Time signature 2/4. Commence 3rd position, R foot *devant*, R hand on hip.
anacrusis. Bend L knee, raising L heel from floor.
1. Strike L heel on floor raising R foot to L ankle.
and. (i.e. next quarter beat). Brush R foot forwards to rest R heel momentarily on floor and immediately draw R foot backwards to level of L ankle and during this accent beat on ball of R foot, before pointing R toe downwards and lifting L heel.
2. Strike L heel on floor, holding R foot fully pointed above L ankle.
and. Return R foot to 3rd with stamp.
This last stamp must also be used as the continuation beat for a repeat.

This exercise gives an excellent way of practising the typical beat on the ball or heel of the foot used in character dance.

In classical dance, i.e. *battement frappé*, the working foot is at the back or front of the supporting leg. But in character dance, the beats must be heard to come from the ball of the working and the heel of the supporting foot. From such an exercise a number of dances can be built (e.g. Sailor's, gipsy and Spanish dance).

Particular attention must be paid to the timing of each beat.

3. EXERCISES WITH THE WORKING LEG RAISED FREELY IN THE AIR.

(i.e. in contrast to *battements tendus* where the foot is usually in full contact with the floor.)

These exercises must be introduced early in training in order to obtain a light, easy and loose lifting movement. They are usually called Medium *Battements*.

This term is borrowed from the old terminology of classical dance which uses *Battements frappés* at 25°. But there is a clear distinction between classical and character medium *battements*. The very term *frappé* indicates that there must be a very clear accent of the turned-out foot along the floor. In character dance the accent must not be "away" but "towards" oneself. This is particularly important for such movements as the character *flic-flac*.

No. 1.

Time signature 2/4. Commence in 3rd, R foot *devant*, R hand on hip.
anacrusis. Raise R leg sideways, toe pointed at 25°.
1. Bending L knee, brush R leg inwards across front of L calf, accenting beat by brushing ball of foot on floor. L leg must be held absolutely straight.
and. Open R leg outwards as at beginning to 25°.
2. Bending R knee, brush R leg inwards as before but raising it behind L calf.
and. Again open R leg out as at beginning.

It is most important that the student uses the working leg freely and accurately, but without showing any movement elsewhere. The swing comes in and out from a fully turned-out knee and toe only, the turnout indicated by the thigh line. The beat of the ball of the foot on the floor must be clear and sharp.

Repeat at least 8 times with each leg.

Once this is mastered it should be rapidly developed and amalgamated with the following:

No. 2.

Time signature 2/4. Commence 3rd, R foot *devant*, R hand on hip.
anacrusis. Prepare as for No. 1 above.

EXERCISES AT THE BARRE

1. Repeat as No. 1, but hold working foot more tensely and do not raise high, only to ankle level.
and. Beat ball of R foot again on floor immediately lifting it to level of L knee before opening it sideways to 25°.
2 and. Repeat as 1-and, but brushing and lifting R foot behind L.

In this exercise the supporting leg is not held as firmly as in No. 1, but has a slightly relaxed knee so that a small *demi-plié* appears as the working foot comes across the ankle after it is beaten on the floor.

This exercise should be repeated 8–16 times with each foot.

Double Flicks. (another form of medium *battements*.)

No. 3.
Time signature 2/4. Commence in 3rd. R foot *devant*, R hand on hip.
anacrusis. Sharply raise R foot so that heel rests just above L ankle. R foot must not be tense.

Bar 1.
1. Brush R foot strongly forwards and with light accent place ball of foot on floor in 4th *devant*.
2. Bring R foot back to front of L ankle, bending R knee.

Bar 2.
Raise R foot a little then brush strongly sideways and with light accent place ball of foot on floor in 2nd position.

Bars 3–4.
Repeat above moving working foot to 4th *derrière* and then again to 2nd position.

19

When the foot moves behind it is not necessary to demand a perfect 4th; as it is essential that the accent is heard, the foot will only move as far as possible because of the shortening required to achieve the sound. The knee must not be bent. Two sharp sounds must be heard, the brush along the floor and the sharp accent of the ball of the foot on the floor. That is a *double flick*.

Begin teaching this exercise at a very slow tempo in order to obtain both sounds. It is a mistake to begin too fast and smudge the sounds. The whole should be repeated 8–16 times with each foot during the first lessons.

No. 4.
During the second year the above must be practised so that on each movement of the R foot, the L heel is raised and lowered, the L knee being kept bent throughout.

No. 5. Double flick front and back.
Time signature 2/4. Commence 3rd, R foot *devant*, R hand on hip.
anacrusis. Bend R knee and raise R foot to rest just above front of L ankle.

Bar 1.
1. Brush R foot strongly forwards and with light accent place R foot on floor 4th *devant*.
and. Lightly bend L knee raising L heel from floor simultaneously bringing R foot back and round behind L ankle. i.e. *petit battement*.
2. Brush R foot strongly backwards and place ball of foot on floor in 4th *derrière*.
and. Lightly bend L knee, raising L heel from floor, simultaneously bringing R foot back behind L ankle.

Bar 2.
1. Stamp ball of R foot on floor behind L without straightening knees.
and. Stamp L heel on floor raising R foot behind L ankle.

EXERCISES AT THE BARRE

2. With a stamp place R foot in 3rd behind L, straightening both knees.
and. Pause.
Repeat in reverse.
This exercise should be repeated 4–8 times with each foot.

The body takes some part in this exercise inclining slightly backwards when the working foot moves *double flick* forwards and forwards when the working foot moves backwards.

The R arm can also take part opening to the side and returning to the hip as the R foot moves forwards and returns to place before being carried across the body almost to the L hip and returning to place as the R foot moves backwards. It also returns to place every time the R foot stamps. i.e. on the R hip.

Preparation for Beaten Jumps.
Time signature 2/4. Commence in 3rd, R foot *devant*, R hand on hip.
anacrusis. Lift R foot with knee bent and twist it inwards across L. Toe is level with L ankle.

Bar 1.
1. Perform a *double flick croisé devant* R foot, and as leg stretches forwards, turn body and head slightly towards left, bending L knee.
and. Draw R foot with knee bent towards L ankle, turning R knee outwards and make slight spring off L, which descends with slight stamp. Body and head return to original position.
2. Perform a *double flick devant*.
and. Repeat and, as above.

Bar 2.
1. Perform a *double flick* to 2nd position.
and. Draw R foot with knee bent towards and behind L ankle. At the same time raise and lower L foot with slight spring and stamp. Body inclines to

CHARACTER DANCE

the right, but head turns to the left. The exercise can be finished in two different ways:

A. 2. Lower R foot to floor with stamp on ball of foot behind L. Do not lower heel and keep knees bent.

and. Raise L foot lightly and replace in position with clear stamp, raising R' foot as in anacrusis above.

B. 2. Stamp R foot behind L.

and. Make half turn raising L foot as in anacrusis above to repeat exercise on opposite side.

This exercise should be repeated 8 times with each foot.

4. VEYER, *i.e. a beaten jump.*

Time signature 2/4. Commence R *devant* (3rd position), R hand on hip.

anacrusis. Raise R foot, knee bent and turn it inwards so that toe rests across L ankle.

Bar 1.

1. Hop and accent hop on descent on ball of L foot, raising R leg sharply straightened to *croisé devant*, toe and knee absolutely straight. Body and head incline to the left.

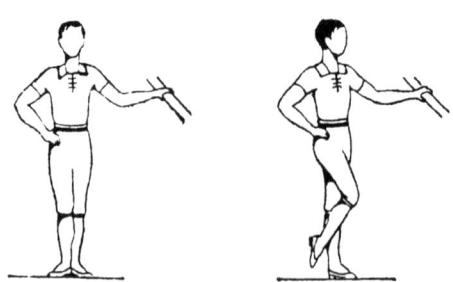

EXERCISES AT THE BARRE

2. Again hop and accent hop on ball of L foot, at the same time return R foot back to L ankle, but immediately thrust it out again straight forwards. Return body and head to erect position.

Bar 2.
1. Repeat hop and accent on L as above, thrusting R foot sideways with *double flick*.
2. Repeat hop and accent on L as above, but bring R foot back into position behind L. Both knees are bent, body easily inclined to right and head turned to left.

The hops on L foot must be swift and sharp. The L knee always being slightly bent.

This exercise can sometimes change during the second bar:
1. R foot does not perform *double flick*, but is thrust out to the side and on
2. returns with a jump into 3rd, where it rests after an accented step on the ball of the foot.

The exercise should be repeated 8 times with each foot, or it can be combined with No. 12, each section being danced 4 times on each side.

5. FLIC-FLAC.

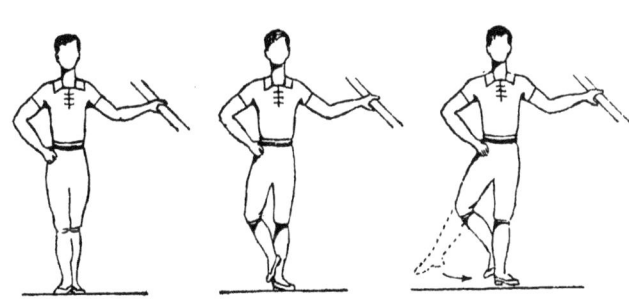

No. 1.

Time signature 2/4. Commence 3rd, R foot *devant*, R hand on hip.
anacrusis. Raise R foot *sur le cou de pied*, but do not tense foot.
1. Brush R foot outwards sideways lightly scraping floor and immediately swing it back with a slightly louder accent on ball of foot as it scrapes the floor behind L ankle.
and. Pause.
2. and. Repeat above, but swinging R leg outwards and inwards in front of L ankle.

It is essential when commencing this exercise to get an accurate beat – out-in – the stronger movement being inwards and the slight pause at the completion of the swing. It should be performed 8 times with each foot.

No. 2. (This is a later development and in the purely theatrical form.)

Time signature 2/4. Commence 3rd position, R foot *derrière*, R hand on hip.
anacrusis. Half bending R knee raise and turn R leg inwards so that foot is level with L ankle.

Bar 1.
1. Brush R leg *croisé devant* with strong accent on floor and straighten leg.
and. Pause.
2. With another brush along floor, turn R leg outwards bending knee and return it so that foot rests fully pointed across front of L calf.
and. Pause.

EXERCISES AT THE BARRE

Bar 2.
1. R foot *double flick* sideways.
and. Raise L heel from floor and lower it with clear beat, bringing R foot, knee bent behind L ankle. (It is not pointed, L knee is bent.)
2. Stamp ball R foot lightly behind L.
and. Straighten both knees. Or raise R leg as in anacrusis above. Repeat 4 to 8 times with each foot.

The principal object of this exercise is to obtain a light and easy turning in and out of the working leg. The positions of the body and head are particularly important. On the first half beat the L shoulder and head incline and turn to the left. On the third half beat the position does not change, but on the fourth half beat the body inclines to the right and the head turns to the left.

No. 3. With a hop.

This *flic-flac* should be performed with a hop on the L foot. It occurs just after the working foot has been accented and is being replaced on the ball of the foot. The hop must be done without any apparent movement elsewhere in the body. It must be swift, clean and well-accented.

This exercise can be used as in No. 2 or in combination with Nos: 1 and 2, and should be performed no more than 4 times with each foot.

No. 4.

Time signature 2/4. Commence R *sur le cou de pied devant*.
anacrusis. R foot *flic-flac devant*, i.e. brushes out and in front of L leg.

Bar 1.
1. Drop on R foot in 3rd raising L foot fully pointed with knee bent behind R. Weight of body is fully on R with knee bent.
and. Pause.
2. Stamp L with straight knee 3rd, raising R foot and straightening body.
and. R foot *flic-flac* sideways.

Bar 2.
Repeat 1 as above.
and. Pause.
2. Repeat 2 as above.

It is important to practise this exercise 8 times on each foot. N.B. It always concludes with a stamp on R foot on last half beat when R foot is working and on L foot when L foot leads.

After the preparatory *flic-flac* the *demi-plié* must be soft and easy so that the weight of the body transfers easily from one foot to the other.

No. 5.
This exercise is as No. 4, but should be practised so that the L foot performs 2 light beats before taking weight on the second beat. The first beat is done on the ball of the foot and the second on the whole foot as the weight is changed.

No. 6.
Time signature 2/4. Commence as No. 3.
anacrusis. Repeat as for No. 3.
1. Hop on ball of L foot bending knee and leaving R foot *sur le cou de pied*.
and. Lower ball of R foot in 3rd position in front of L, raising L foot *sur le cou de pied* behind R.
2. Step on L behind R, raising R *sur le cou de pied*.
and. *Flic-flac* sideways R and continue as above.

The knees must be kept easily bent during this exercise and the body must not appear to move with the change of weight and feet. This is particularly important during the hop on the L foot.

As soon as this is mastered it should be combined with Nos. 4 and 5.

No. 7. Flic-Flac with an inward twist of the foot.
All the above *flic-flac* exercises can be strengthened by using an inward twist of the working foot. This twist is made during the brushing of the foot forwards i.e. during the *flic* and then outwards during the *flac* or the drawing of the foot backwards. Thus during the whole *flic-flac* the R (or L) leg must turn easily inwards and immediately outwards from the hip-joint. This way of performing the *flic-flac* can be used in exercises Nos. 4, 5, 6 but only when the movement is to the front. It should not be practised until all the other *flic-flacs* have been mastered.

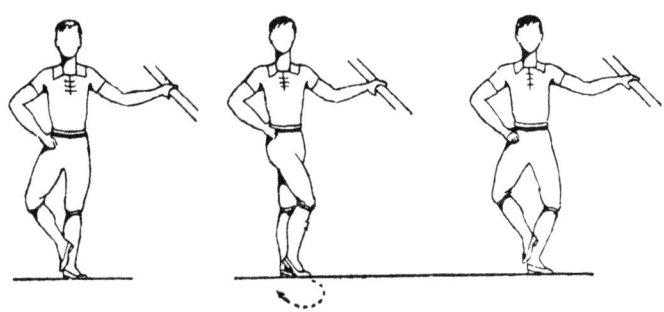

6. EXERCISES ON DRUMMING.

Drumming plays an important part in many character dances and there are unlimited variations.

The particular character of the *drumming* in certain dances is discussed in the second half of this book although it must also play a valuable part in training at the barre. Only these latter principles are discussed here.

The basic principle of *drumming* lies in the quick action of the tap of the foot on the floor and the interplay between the heel and *demi-pointe*. *Flic-flac* can suggest *drumming*, but *drumming* has its own exclusive quality. The family likeness between the two is only auditory. In a *flic-flac* the foot brushes the floor only in a passing movement as it is made with a relaxed foot. In *drumming* the foot must be controlled and the stamp on the floor must sound clearly as it marks the firm beat of the movement.

Drumming No. 1.
Time signature 2/4. Commence 3rd position.
anacrusis. Raise R foot bent to level of L ankle.
1. Stamp whole R foot on floor in 3rd *devant* raising L foot behind R ankle.
and. Stamp *demi-pointe* behind R and raise it again behind R ankle.
2. Stamp L foot in position raising R foot to level of L ankle.
and. Without straightening knee, strike R *demi-pointe* in front of foot and continue as before.

No. 2.
Time signature 3/4. Commence in 3rd position.
anacrusis as in No. 1 above.

EXERCISES AT THE BARRE

1. As in No. 1 above.
2. As in – and – above.
3. Repeat last stamp.
Repeat movement commencing L foot behind R and continue.

No. 3.
Time signature 2/4. Commence in 3rd position.
anacrusis. As in No. 1 above.
1. As in No. 1.
and. Stamp L *demi-pointe* twice behind R and again raise it behind R ankle.
2. Stamp L foot behind R in 3rd position and raise R foot to L ankle.
and. Repeat as in – and – above but using R *demi-pointe* in front of L.

The first exercise must be studied very early to be followed by No. 2 but the third which should be danced at the fastest possible speed should not be attempted until the student has acquired the necessary technical facility.

Before repeating Nos. 1, 2, 3 in the centre they should be given a theatrical form namely: the first stamp on the R foot should be made in 3rd position and with a small step forwards *éffacé* and on the second stamp return to 3rd position. During the second stamp the body should incline slightly backwards with the L shoulder lowered, but as the foot returns to 3rd, the body bends slightly forwards (without rounding the line of the spine) with the R shoulder slightly lowered.

When these exercises are practised after being mastered at the barre, particularly when taken in the centre, the arms should be held or moved in one or another theatrical style (e.g. as in Spanish dance).

No. 4.
Time signature 2/4. Commence 3rd position. R foot *devant*.
anacrusis. Raise L heel, knee slightly bent from the floor.
1. Stamp L heel, raising R heel, knee bent to L ankle.
and. Stamp R heel again raising L heel.
2. Repeat stamp on L heel but raise R foot behind L heel.
and. Stamp R foot in 3rd position behind L, raising L heel from floor and continue as above.

The entire exercise must be performed with relaxed and slightly bent knees. It should be taught early and repeated 8–16 times.

No. 5.
Another valuable exercise based on the above uses an inner turn of the foot. i.e.:
Repeat No. 4. once then continue:
1, – and. Repeat as in No. 4.
2. Stamp L heel on floor at the same time raising R foot to L ankle and turning R knee inwards.
and. Stamp R foot placing it besides L with feet straight and both pointing sideways to the audience.

If the L foot makes a small stamp to the left (i.e. moves on the whole foot and not on the *demi-pointes*, there will be a slight movement to the left), then a true dance movement is made typical of Russian dance. In this case, the arm should also take on a typical Russian form.

No. 6.
This is performed with *Battement Tendu* No. 3.

In this variation after the two stamps of the first bar No. 4 which are behind and in front (or in reverse). Place R heel out sideways. This stamp can either be on the R heel or whole foot and is accompanied by a stamp on the L heel. The R foot moving to the side can be taken with the toe turned up or down, in front or behind.

No. 7.
This is a combination of *Battement tendu* No. 5 with *Drumming* No. 4. In which the number of stamps on the R foot is increased to four. It should not be tried until all the above exercises are mastered and then practised 4–8 times.

It is important never to stretch the knees fully in this exercise.

No. 8. (This is known as the Drum Roll.)
Time signature 2/4. Commence 3rd position, R *devant* and knees slightly bent.

Bar 1.
anacrusis. Raise L heel by bending knee.
1. Stamp L heel, raising R foot upwards parallel to floor.
and. Pause.

EXERCISES AT THE BARRE

2. Stamp R heel on floor in place.
and. Change weight from R heel to ball of R foot (without moving knee) and raising L heel from floor.

Bar 2.
1. Repeat 1. above.
and. Pause.
2. Stamp R foot in 3rd position.
Repeat whole.

This must be performed lightly. It can also be performed with an inward turn of the R leg. It should be practised from 8–16 times Such movements are typical of Russian dance and have more difficult forms. In Russian dance they are usually most complicated, the final stamp very often taking place after the change from heel to toe has been performed 3 times. This should be practised first at the barre.

No. 9. The most difficult form of Drumming.
Time signature 2/4. Commence 3rd position.

Bar 1.
1. Stamp L heel raising R foot parallel to the floor.
and. Pause.
2. Stamp R *demi-pointes*.
and. With stamp transfer weight from *demi-pointe* to R heel, toes raised upwards and L heel also raised.

Bar 2.
1. Stamp L heel raising R foot to L ankle.
and. Pause.
2. Stamp R foot in 3rd position.
Repeat whole from 8–16 times.

This exercise as No 8 must be practised gradually getting faster and thus taking 1 and not 2 bars of music.

No. 10.
This is the same as above but the final stamp is only made after three changes of weight from *demi-pointes* to the heels have been made. It should be danced not more than 8 times. As with the preceding exercises it can be varied by turning the foot inwards and outwards before the final stamp.

No. 11. This is a typical basic step for a Spanish character walk.
Time signature 2/4. Commence feet together pointing straight forwards and knees slightly bent.
anacrusis. Raise R foot parallel to the floor knee slightly bent and L leg straight.

Bar 1.
1. Stamp R *demi-pointe* on floor without stretching knee fully and raise L foot parallel to floor and level with L ankle.
and. Stamp L heel making slight movement forwards so that heel comes to level of R instep. R foot remains on *demi-pointe,* knee bent. L toes are slightly raised upwards.
2. Repeat 1 using L foot but moving slightly backwards, i.e. to preparatory position and raising R foot from floor.
and. Repeat – and – with R foot but do not change its position.

Bar 2.
1. Lower L heel with stamp, raising R foot parallel to the floor.
and. Stamp R *demi-pointe* and transfer weight to heel, raising R toes and L heel.

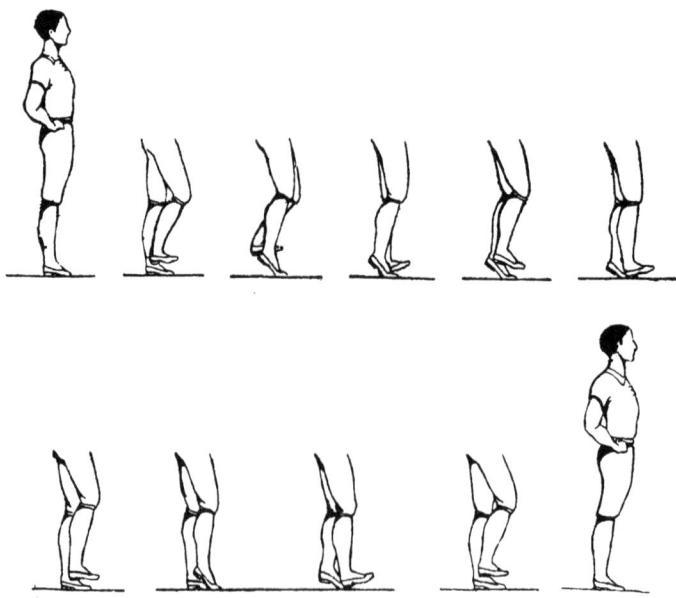

2. Stamp L heel, raising R foot.
and. Stamp R foot back into preparatory position, straightening knees.

This exercise is the basis of many Spanish dances on stage. It should be studied at the barre and in the centre. From this type of movement it is comparatively easy to establish the theatrical form by insisting on Spanish style stance, head and arms when working in the centre.

7. PAS TORTILLES. *Or Inwards and Outwards movements.*

No. 1.
Time signature 2/4. Commence R foot raised to side at 15°. Leg straight, toe pointed.
1. Bring R toe inwards, bending R knee through 5th position and across in front of L until toe rests on floor just past L toe – both knees easily bent.
and. Without lifting R toe, turn knee inwards and lower L heel. Both feet are now parallel R in front of L.
2. Without raising foot, slide R backwards to 2nd position. (R foot is turned inwards) raising R heel and easily bending L knee a little further.
and. Turn R foot outwards pointing toe, thus both legs are returned to the preparatory position.

This exercise must be performed very carefully as many mistakes can arise. For a perfect performance of 1. the leg must be fully turned-out before it is fully turned inwards from the hip without any body movement. on 2. the whole foot must slide backwards along the floor fully turned-in before raising the heel from the floor. It is essential to work through the whole foot throughout this exercise. It should be practised 8–16 times with each foot. From this is developed the following more complicated variation.

No. 2.
Time signature 2/2. Commence as No. 1. above.
1. and. Repeat as above.
2. Raise R toe and turn leg outwards on heel then replace toe on floor.
and. Raise R leg fully stretched sideways as in preparatory position.

The particular value of this exercise is to increase the activity of the foot. In No. 1. the change from *en dehors* to *en dedans* and back must be exact. It must defined at a quick tempo. It can also be danced together with No. 1 and up to 8 times with each foot.

No. 3.
This is a theatrical form of the above and is an introduction to the small Hungarian *battements* in the most conventional form and in other movements which occur in French and other dances.
Time signature 3/4. Commence as in Nos. 1 and 2 but do not return to the preparatory opening of the leg after the first two beats. Now continue:
and. Turn R foot inwards from hip lowering heel and turning leg outwards to the right.
3. Lower R toes moving into 2nd position, *demi-plié*.
and. Open R leg into preparatory position.

The last turn of the foot can also be done very swiftly. Repeat 8–16 times and also practise in 2/4 time signature.

As already noted the turning point in and out of the foot can be doubled and trebled as the students progress. Later with the first brush across of the working foot the body can incline to the same side without inclining or bending the back. Other movements are possible, e.g. with the first brush of the working foot, the body can incline towards the supporting leg, then returns to normal as the working foot moves *en dehors*. In the first case the head glances towards the toes of the working foot and in the second, the head follows the movement of the body. When these two movements are combined a third variation results and all three should be practised as early as possible.

No. 4.
Time signature 2/4. Commence as in No. 1.
1. Raise and turn R leg inwards, knee bent at right angles, toes fully pointed, L leg straight.
and. Stamp R foot turned inwards forwards and in front of L (i.e. feet are parallel and about one foot apart), both knees slightly bent.
2. Raise R leg, knee bent and turned outwards before stamping it in 3rd position. At this moment straighten both knees slightly.
and. Return R foot to preparatory position.

It is essential to practise this exercise 8 times with each foot; the movements of the head and body are the same as in No. 3. And here several mistakes can arise. The movement in the hips must be sharp and minimal. It is not smooth but clear and energetic with strong accents.

No. 5.
Time signature 3/4. Commence as in No. 1.
1 – and 2. As 1 – and 2 No:4. then continue:
and. Raise R foot again to level of L ankle and turn inwards, then with a sharp stamp place R foot a little apart from L.
3. As in No. 4.
and. Return to preparatory position.

This exercise must be introduced in the simplest and slowest form before working it up to the correct speed. Therefore, together with other exercises aiming to develop a strong action of the foot and knee, it is essential to introduce other movements and ultimately introduce wider movements using the whole leg (as in *Grands battements* in Hungarian style).

It is evident from the above analysis the exercise must be performed to 3/4 time signature. The teacher's problem is to develop the speed until it can be performed to 2/4. It is therefore necessary to beat accurately so that it can eventually be performed double time.

All the above exercises known as *Pas Tortillés* (with the exception of No. 1.) have a very particular function. They are all danced from beginning to end with the L foot on the highest *demi-pointes*. Thus the L or supporting leg has only one movement. A form of *fondu* together with the contrary *relevé*. This group of movements has only one function, to hop on the supporting leg. It thus gives strength and depending on its accuracy, finish both to the beginning and end of the step.

The hop is simultaneous with the lift of the R foot into the preparatory position. The L knee lightly bends before the hop, but during the hop the knee and toes are stretched. The L foot returns to the floor with the first movement of the R foot.

In order not to tire the supporting leg it is essential to create *enchainements* in which this foot is used in various ways, i.e. flat foot, *demi-pointes* and hopping, and in various degrees of difficulty. A general mistake is to allow the shaking of the body during the hop in order to make it higher. It is not useful to heighten the hop as this only shakes the line of the body making it look comic. The body must be held strongly and as still as possible at all times.

8. CIRCLING OF THE LEGS, *i.e. Ronds de Jambe.*

There are two forms of this type of movement. First the foot circles on the floor or in the air. Second is the circling of the leg on the floor or in the air.

As the circling of the foot is the close relation of the *pas tortillés* above, it is necessary to introduce these fairly early.

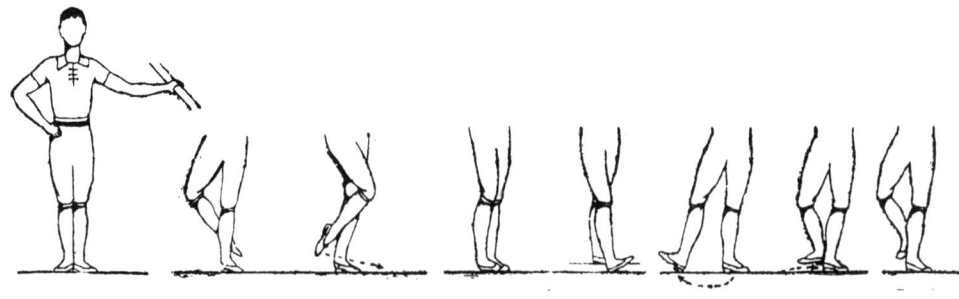

EXERCISES AT THE BARRE

No. 1. Rond de pied à terre.
Time signature 2/4. Commence 1st position.
anacrusis. Lightly bend R knee and raise until ankle rests behind and across L ankle. Knee is turned-out.
1. Twist and turn R knee inwards so that it rests across L knee, R toe fully pointed, then brush R foot on floor besides L foot and place R heel on floor just in front of L toe. (R toe is turned upwards.)
and. Circle R heel outwards through 4th to 2nd position and bring it back behind L heel.
2. R heel will now be lifted behind L ankle and foot returns to position as on anacrusis above.
Repeat above.

The entire movement must be performed smoothly and without any movement of the L leg. Moderate tempo. It should be repeated from 8–16 times with each foot.

It is interesting to note that together with the circling movement of the foot, there is a very full turning out of the leg from the hip-joint. This is vital in the performance, although it is called circling of the foot. Therefore it must be practised very carefully with each foot, and there must be the minimum stress on the action of the hip, which must remain still throughout.

No. 2. Circling and Turning on the Foot of the Supporting Leg.
Repeat as above but move the L foot as follows:
1. Scarcely raising the L heel from the floor turn L toe inwards.
and. Turn L toe outwards.

The heel will be seen to turn in and out. When using this movement it is essential to keep the knee of the supporting leg absolutely straight and make the minimum amount of movement at the hip. Students always make the mistake of using too much movement in the hip in order to bring the R knee across and thus spoil the total style of the movement. The body plays an important part in maintaining style, therefore it must be calm and erect. The L leg must not be stiff, but easily held straight.

The exercises should be practised 8 times without and 8 times with the movement of the supporting leg.

No. 3. Rond de pied en l'air.
This should not be practised until the circling of the foot on the floor becomes automatic. Once mastered the movement must be practised the foot making the same circle in the air. The foot should not be raised too high, but only far enough for the foot to be seen to be away from the floor. The L foot is held or moved as in No. 2. The theatrical effect of this movement is used in sailor's dances and is made very strongly and precisely.

The above *ronds à terre* are used a great deal and the following variations must also be added.

No. 4. Character rond de jambe.
Time signature 2/4. Commence in 1st position.
anacrusis. Bend R knee and raise foot fully pointed behind L ankle, then twist R knee inwards across L without displacing hips.
1. Drop outside of R foot just in front and beside L and continue movement by pushing R toe diagonally across in front of L.
and. Circle R toe (as in classical *rond de jambe*) forwards and round to back.
2. Bend R toe behind L ankle with well-turned-out knee.
and. Turn R knee inwards as on anacrusis above.

Repeat 8 times with each foot. Commence in tempo moderato, then gradually quicken.

As in No. 1. This *rond de jambe* can also be performed to 3/4 and this is valuable during the first stages of practise as it allows for a more detailed analysis. The basic problem is to perform the movement smoothly yet with precision so that the placing of the R foot beside the L has a short sharp accent, but does not break the continuity of the action.

No. 5.
This second variant of the above is not so loose as classical *rond de jambe*. In the above the dancer places the outside edge of the foot on the ground before stretching the working leg *pointe tendue* diagonally across and in front of the other, and then circles the fully pointed foot *en dehors* to the back. In this version the movement commences as above, but after the working foot is placed by the side of the other, the leg is stretched diagonally across and in front until the heel rests on the floor and is circled *en dehors* to the back, before the toe is stretched downwards as the leg is raised behind the supporting leg. After this exercise has been mastered it should be combined with No. 4. I.e. repeat No. 4. 8 times and then No. 5. 8 times.

EXERCISES AT THE BARRE

No. 6.
Time signature 4/4. Commence in 3rd or normal position.
1. Stretch R *pointe dendue devant* simultaneously sinking on L to lowest *fondu*. Having reached lowest point, stretch and reverse R foot so that heel rests on the floor.
2. Circle R leg to side on heel.
3. Circle R leg to back gradually pointing toe but without bending R knee.
4. Slowly rise bringing R foot to 3rd *derrière*, or normal position.
   Repeat in reverse.

This should be repeated 4 times only with each foot. It is a heavy exercise and one of the most difficult. The problem is to retain the weight over the supporting leg *fondu*, whilst keeping the working leg moving slowly and smoothly.

9. VEREVOCHKA.

CHARACTER DANCE

No. 1.
Time signature 2/4. Commence 3rd position.
anacrusis. Sharply raised R leg knee bent to 90°, toe should rest in front of L knee.
1. Return R foot to 3rd position *devant*.
and. Repeat as above.
2. Pass R toe behind L knee and lower R foot to 3rd *derrière*.
   Repeat 8–16 times on both feet used alternately.

No. 2.
Repeat No. 1. rising on *demi-pointe* each time the R leg is lifted.

No. 3.
Repeat with a small hop on all but fully stretched supporting leg.

No. 4.
At a later stage in training the hop should be made with the supporting leg well bent. This movement is done in such a way that the level of the head remains more or less at the same height throughout.

No. 5.
Time signature 2/4. Commence in 3rd position.
anacrusis. Raise and turn R leg inwards bent at knee to 90°, toe level with L knee front, then immediately turn it outwards.

EXERCISES AT THE BARRE

Bar 1.
1. Replace R in 3rd *devant* with light stamp clicking it against L heel.
and. Immediately raise R knee turned-out to the same height as before and turn it inwards keeping toe against L knee.
2. Drop R foot as before with a slight click against L heel, but feet are now in normal position, i.e. both legs are slightly turned towards the barre.
and. Repeat from anacrusis and 1st bar as above during *Bar 2*.
   Repeat 8 times with each foot.

No. 6.
When the above has been mastered, it should be practised with a hop on the supporting leg each time the working leg is raised and twisted inwards and outwards on the anacrusis.

10. CHARACTER BATTEMENTS FONDUS.

No. 1.
Time signature 3/4. Commence by rising on L *demi-pointe* and raising R leg fully stretched sideways to 45°, open R and to 2nd.
anacrusis. Still standing on L *demi-pointe*, whip R foot behind L calf, then twist R leg, knee bent inwards and *fondu* by dropping L heel.
1. Twist R leg outwards maintaining *fondu*.
2. Stretch R leg outwards rising on L *demi-pointe*.
3. Hold.
   Repeat 8 times on each side.

No. 2.
The above exercise should also be practised raising the working leg to 90° and making several changes in the placing of the body as in the following example:

anacrusis. Raise R leg bent so that toe is behind L knee, twist R leg inwards with *fondu* on L and drop L heel simultaneously circling R arm upwards to 3rd and downwards in front of body which bends towards barre.
1. Straightening body, twist R leg outwards, knee bent, toe resting on L knee (L leg *fondu*) and open arm to 2nd.
2. Stretch R leg outwards to 90° simultaneously straightening L knee.
3. Pause.

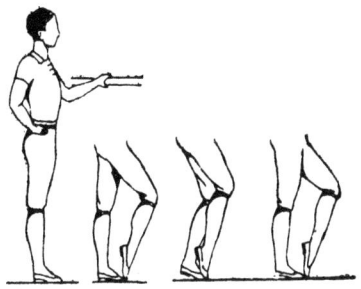

11. PREPARATION FOR KNEE TWISTING.

No. 1.
Time signature 2/4. Commencing in normal position.
1. Bend R knee lifting heel from floor, but without changing position of toe.
2. Replace R heel simultaneously lifting L heel.
  Repeat at least 16 times, gradually increasing speed.

No. 2.
Repeat as No. 1 above but twist working leg inwards as heel is lifted from the floor. Transfer of weight must see the body kept very erect and as still as possible. The twist takes place from the thigh downwards only.

No. 3.
No. 1 should also be practised in the centre with both hands on the hips and body kept *de face* and as still as possible. The bent knees twist alternately across each other on the transfer of weight. The important aspect of this exercise is to ensure that the toes never leave the floor during the transfer of weight, and the toe of each foot always touches the other.

Once both Nos. 2 and 3 have been mastered they should be practised alternately in some *enchainement*.

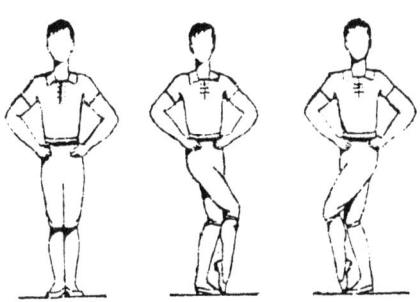

CHARACTER DANCE

12. PREPARATION FOR KHACHALKI. (Rocking).

No. 1.
Time signature 2/4. Commence 3rd position.
anacrusis. Raise R leg sideways to 10°.
1. Brush R foot inwards and fall on to it in 5th position with knee bent, simultaneously raising L heel and inclining body slightly to right.
2. Transfer weight back to L foot straightening knee and body, simultaneously stretching R leg out sideways as preparation for repeat of movement, but bringing R foot behind L.

No. 2.
Time signature 2/4. Prepare as No. 1. above.
1. Repeat as 1 above.
and. Replace L heel but do not stretch knee and simultaneously raise R toe close to L toe inclining body slightly to left.
2. Reverse position of feet.
and. Stretch R leg out sideways, ready to repeat whole.

In both these exercises it is important to emphasize the difference between the erect body for the preparation and its slightly inclined position in the *rock*.

13. HUNGARIAN BATTEMENTS.

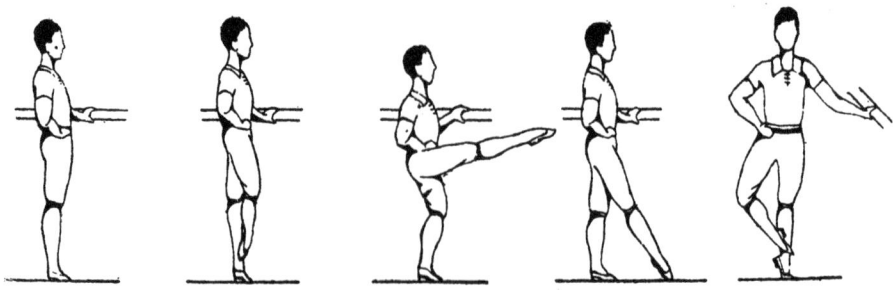

EXERCISES AT THE BARRE

No. 1.
Time signature 4/4. Commence 3rd position, R hand on hip.
anacrusis. Raise R leg knee bent until it is just above L ankle, knee well turned-out.
1. Thrust R leg forwards to 90° simultaneously bending L knee and opening R arm through 1st to 2nd position.
2. Pause and hold.
3. Drop R to *pointe tendue devant* straightening L knee and returning R hand to hip.
4. Bring R foot back *sur le cou de pied* as on anacrusis above but rise on L *demi-pointe*.

Repeat sequence throwing leg out sideways, backwards and sideways again.

No. 2. Battement Développé (staccato).
Time signature 4/4. Commence in 3rd position, hand on hip.
anacrusis. Rise on *demi-pointes,* raising R leg knee bent till toes reach L knee.
1. Thrust R leg out sideways to 90° with strong *fondu* on L marking beat with drop of L heel.
and. Holding R leg steady, lift L heel.

CHARACTER DANCE

2. – and. Still holding R leg, drop L heel firmly.
3. Stretch L leg and rise on *demi-pointe*.
and. Drop L heel strongly keeping L knee straight.
4. Lower R foot behind L.
   Repeat 8 times before repeating on other side.

No. 3.
When No. 2 has been mastered it should be practised with two heel beats on second beat of bar.

No. 4. Battement Développé with Fondu.
Time signature 4/4. Commence in 3rd position, R hand on hip.
anacrusis. Rise on L *demi-pointe* raising R leg knee bent until toe touches L knee.
1. Thrust R leg out sideways to 90° simultaneously sinking L *fondu* and opening R arm to 2nd.
2. Deepen L *fondu* by lifting L heel immediately dropping R heel to floor.
3. Rise on L *demi-pointe* raising R leg to 90°.
4. Lower R to 3rd position as L heel lightly marks beat on floor and close R hand on hip.
   Repeat 4–8 times with each leg.

EXERCISES AT THE BARRE

14. GRANDS BATTEMENTS.

No. 1.
Time signature 4/4. Commence in small 4th position R *derrière* and in *pointe tendue*.

To an absolutely regular rhythm throw R leg forwards on first and third beats to 90° and back again to *pointe tendue derrière*.

Repeat at least 8 times with each leg.

No. 2. Dropping to the knee.
Time signature 4/4. Commence 4th, R *derrière*.
anacrusis. Raise R leg, knee bent and twist it towards then away from the barre, body facing front.

1. Twisting slightly towards barre, swing R leg still bent and simultaneously bending L knee, sink downwards so that –
2. R knee all but rests on floor, being careful to stretch front of R foot on floor and not allowing L heel to rise.
3. Straighten L leg and line of body throwing R leg forwards to 90°.
4. Pass R leg through 1st into *grand battement derrière* and immediately lower foot to small 4th *derrière*.

Repeat 4 times only before repeating on other side. When fully mastered the exercise should be repeated 8 times. (Sketch above is when danced in centre.)

No. 3. With Coupé tombé.
Time signature 2/4. Commence 3rd, R *devant*.
anacrusis. Throw R leg upwards and forwards to 90° as in any classical *battement*.
1. *Tombé* R into 3rd position simultaneously lifting L foot, knee bent and toe pointed across bottom of R calf.
and. Drop L foot in 3rd with sharp stamp, immediately raising R leg as on anacrusis above.

Repeat this movement 8–16 times with each foot.

The exercise can also be practised throwing the leg out sideways to 90°. It is not performed to the back.

No. 4. Balancé with Lunge.
Time signature 2/4. Commence 1st position, R arm in 2nd.
anacrusis. Throw R leg upwards and forwards to 90°.

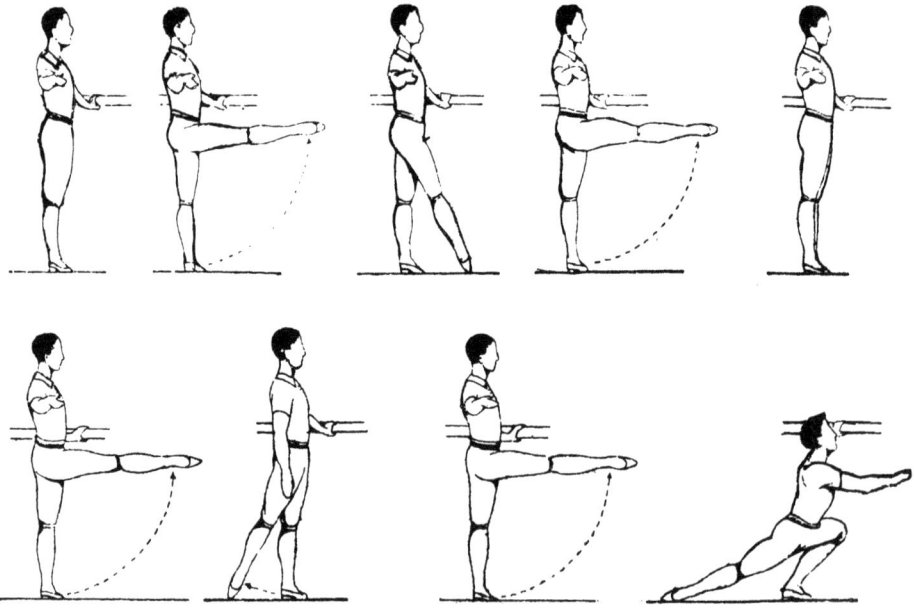

EXERCISES AT THE BARRE

Bar 1.
1. Drop R to *pointe tendue devant*.
and. Throw leg upwards again.
2. Lower R leg to 1st position.
and. Throw R leg upwards.

Bar 2.
1. Lower R leg to *pointe tendue derrière*, passing it through 1st.
and. Throw R upwards and forwards again.
2. Lower R leg passing it through 1st and stretching it with toe fully pointed, simultaneously sink into lowest *fondu* on L, as R arm moves through to 1st position and body inclines forwards, i.e. the dancer is in a lunge position with all the weight over the supporting leg.
and. The movement is now repeated from anacrusis above.

This exercise should only be given to boys' classes. It can be varied once it is mastered.

No. 5.
Same as above but rise on *demi-pointe* with throw of leg forwards before lunge.

No. 6.
Same as above but bring R leg down on heel with *fondu* on L on first beat of bar.

15. REVOLTADE.

No. 1.
Time signature 2/4. Commence in 3rd, R *devant*, both hands on barre.
1. *Flick battement croisé devant* with straight R leg across L *fondu*.
and. Spring off L, bending knee and bringing foot over R, which must be held still.
2. Drop on L *fondu*, simultaneously lowering R so that R foot rests just behind L ankle.
and. *Coupé* ready to repeat with L foot.
Repeat 8 times in all.

When first practised the exercise should be danced slowly then gradually quickened before being tried in the centre.

No. 2. Triple Flick.
This movement consist of one *flick battement* and 3 *revoltades*, i.e. *Flick battement* as No. 1 above followed by 3 *revoltades* always springing off L (or R) foot passing it in front, behind and then in front before repeating the exercise with the other foot.

16. HOLUBETZ. Small Cabrioles, or clips.

No. 1.
Time signature 3/4. Commence in normal position.
anacrusis. Raise L foot, knee very slightly bent as far as R ankle.

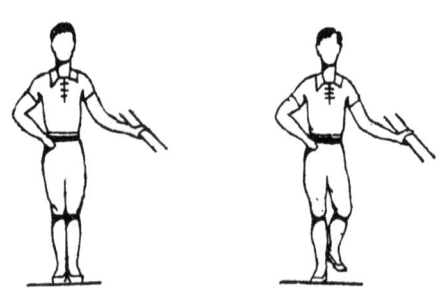

EXERCISES AT THE BARRE

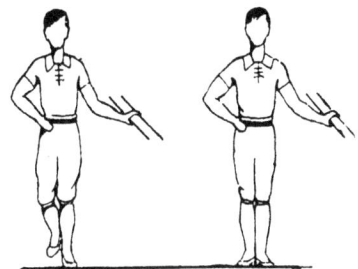

1. Stamp L foot on floor lifting R heel from floor and twisting leg slightly inwards on toe.
2. Return R to preparatory position with clear beat on side of L heel.
3. Lift R foot slightly from floor and stamp in 6th position.

This should be practised 8 times before repeating with other foot. It is essential that the leg action is as strong as possible, but never exaggerated. The body must be kept as still as possible.

No. 2. Double Holubetz (or clip) on one foot.
Time signature 2/4. Commence in 6th position.

Bar 1.
1. Slightly raise L foot before stamping it clearly as R foot *clips* against L heel.
2. Repeat 2 as in No. 1 above.

Bar 2.
1. *Clip* R foot again on side on L heel.
2. Stamp R foot.

This exercise can also be performed with a triple *clip* if the time signature is changed to 3/4.

Introduction to Studies in Character Dance

Before starting to study the particular steps on any one country it is important to note those steps which constantly appear no matter where the dancer is performing. These are known by the titles common to classical dance, yet in every case are coloured by the music, characteristics and particular style of the country in whose dance they appear.

1. Pas de Basque.
The sketch above gives some idea of the varying qualities to be found in a. b. Georgian; c. Polovtsian Dance of Prince Igor; d. Le Corsaire; e. Jota Aragonesa; f. Cossack; g. Negro slave in Cléopatra.

The following sketch gives yet another view of a *grand pas de basque* from Petipa's *Le Roi Candaule* while that below shows the *grand pas de basque en tournant* in Fokine's choreography of *Prince Igor*.

2. Pas de Bourrée.

The *pas de bourrée* originated in the folk dances of Auvergne where it is still danced but unlike the usual classical version the first step and accent is downwards. The sketch below from an old version of *La Fille Mal Gardée* gives some idea of the traditional step although the legs are not so turned-out.

3. Balancé or pas de Valse.
This too can take on many colours as it is changed by the musical accents and temperaments of the people dancing.

4. Running on the Stage.
But it is the simple act of running that can be so changed as the following sketches demonstrate.

a. is in the *demi-caractère* style of Petipa's *Le Corsaire*.

b., c. and d. are examples of running to be practised in class; b. the body is directed with long paces and body upright; c. with body directed forwards and d. with head held backwards.

a.

b.

c.   d.

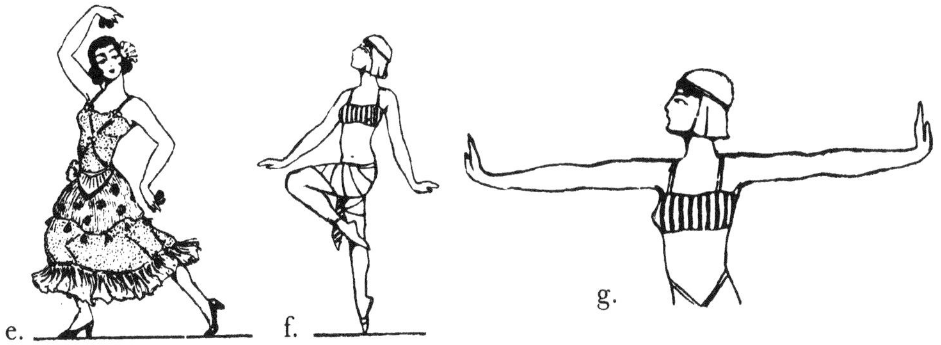

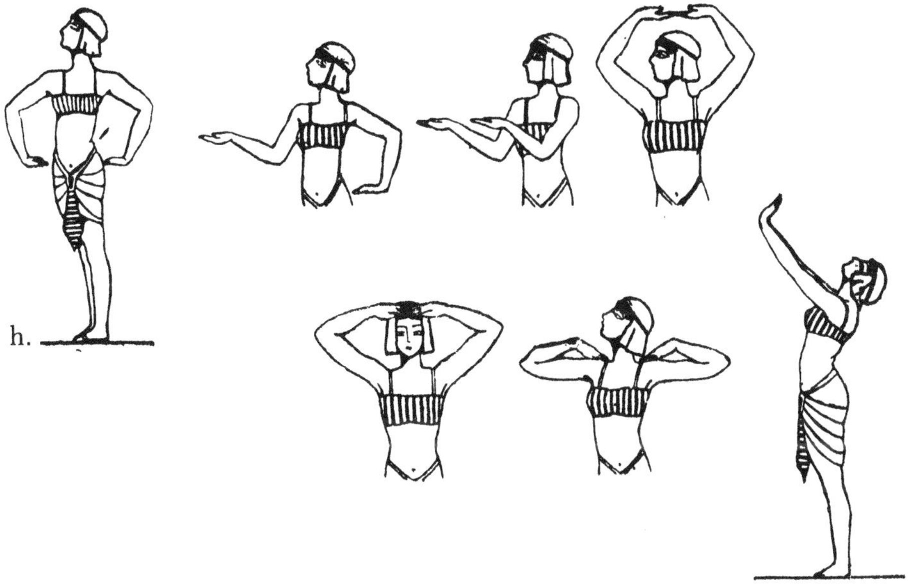

e. is a Spanish run.
f., g. and h. are examples from the Egyptian dances of Fokine's *Cléopatra* whilst i. is the marvellous run of the Polovtsian Warriors in Fokine's *Prince Igor*.

STUDIES

1. Studies in Russian Dance

Unless otherwise stated the time signature for the following exercises is 2/4.

1. Yelochka. No. 1.
Commence 1st position, knees slightly bent.
1. Twist R foot inwards lifting heel slightly but leaving toe *en place*, simultaneously twist L foot inwards leaving heel on floor (i.e. toes of feet are kept together as movement begins and travels to right).
2. Reverse twisting movement returning feet to 1st, but continuing to travel to right.

The movement should appear as if using the whole foot and must be kept very smooth and evenly marked to the beat. The body must be kept as still as possible.

Repeat at least 8 times to right before returning to left. Movement can be travelled in a circle. Arms can be held on hips or in 2nd for boys. Girls can place them on hips, in 2nd, behind their head or using various simple *ports de bras*.

2. Yelochka No. 2.
A somewhat similar movement as above, but the dancer twists both legs in the same direction.
Commence normal position, knees slightly bent.

1. Slightly raise heels from floor, twisting knees and toes to right before replacing them on floor.
2. Now twist knees and heels to right. Continue repeating this movement at least 8 times before repeating movement to left. The body must be kept as still as possible. The twisting movement should be seen to run from the hips downwards. Hands are usually kept on the hips during this step.

3. Drob. (Drumming Walk.) No. 1.

This is the simplest form of *Drumming* walk, i.e. small steps taken with a clear beat of the whole foot on the floor. The foot scarcely leaves the floor or travels very far as the heel is beaten and when the whole foot is placed on the floor it must take the weight of the body so that the other foot is free to make the next beat.

This walk should first be practised very slowly, the tempo then gradually increased until it is performed as fast as possible and in various floor patterns, particularly in figures of eight. It must always look smooth, the body kept as still as possible. This is particularly important when dancing Russian dance on the stage. However if attempting to convey the feeling of peasant dance then the shoulders should be directed towards the line taken.

4. Drob. No. 2.
Commence normal position.
1. Raise R foot, knee slightly bent to level of and just in front of L ankle.
and. Stamp R just in front of L, simultaneously raising L slightly.
2. Stamp L, just in front of R, raising R slightly.
and. Stamp R beside L.

Repeat commencing R foot. Continue as above.

The step can also be performed using L foot. It is never danced using alternate feet. It must always commence with slightly bent knees and can be danced travelling very small distances forwards, *en place*, but it is more usual to dance travelling in a figure of eight. Arms can be held in any appropriate pose. The two most usual are hands on hips, or opened – not too widely – in 2nd.

5. Drob. No. 3.

Commence normal position.
1. Stamp L lightly, slightly raising R, knee bent with sole parallel to the floor.
and. Beat R heel and immediately reverse foot, slightly beating R toe, i.e. lift heel upwards without altering height of leg.
2. Repeat stamp L as on first beat.
and. Stamp R beside L.

Repeat as above, always commencing L foot.

6. Drob. No. 4. (The most advanced form.)

Bar 1.
Repeat as above but on last half beat, beat R heel and immediately reverse foot lightly tapping R toe (i.e. lift R heel).

Bar 2.
Repeat as from first beat above, but on last half beat stamp R foot beside L.

The foot work in any form of *Drob* must be light and crisp and a distinction made between a stamp and a step. These walks are usually performed with *drumming* on the R foot only.

7. Theatrical form of traditional Russian promenade.

Promenade No. 1.

Commence normal position.
anacrusis. With slight *fondu* L, raise R leg stretched and toe pointed slightly from floor.
1. Take small step forwards R, movement going through whole foot and weight carried directly over as L rises from floor.
and. Bring L to R without completely lowering heel.
2. Take another step forwards R, completely lowering heel and slightly bending knee simultaneously stretching L forwards past R, but not raising it high from floor.

Repeat above with L foot.

This *promenade* is danced more or less on *quarter pointes*, the heel being lowered to the floor on the second beat.

8. Traditional Form of Promenade. No. 2. (i.e. used in Folk dance.)

This has the same form as No. 1. but the movement is made on the whole foot, the working one scarcely lifted from the floor. It is commonly used when dancing in circles all girls or all boys, or girls and boys standing alternately. It can be danced in couples linking elbows and dancing round together, or with R arms round each other's waists, L hands on shoulders. The position of the arms must be clearly changed when turning to go the other way.

9. Promenade No. 3. Used to cover more ground.

1. Take small step forwards R.
and. Small step forwards L.
2. Step forwards R raising L, knee bent so that L foot rests beside R ankle.
and. Tiny hop R, skidding along floor a little forwards, L foot held in place. Continue walk with L foot.

Several different *ports de bras* can be used during the *promenade* e.g. hands on hips; arms in 2nd; arms opening on first bar and closing on second bar; arms moving across body in 3rd position using law of opposition.

This walk is often followed by *Verevochka* (see below). The level of the working foot always remaining the same, i.e. to the level of the supporting ankle.

10. Sideways walk.

Commence normal position.
anacrusis. Open and raise L leg slightly sideways, foot flat and level in front of R ankle.

1. Take small step to left pushing L foot into floor with slightly bent knee and weight fully centred over leg, raising R just behind L.
and. Lower R *quarter pointe* behind L without straightening knee and transfer weight momentarily on to R foot.
2–and. Repeat above and continue onwards from 4, 8 or 16 bars. Repeat other side.

In traditional Russian dance this sideways walk is performed very smoothly, with very small, light steps on the whole foot, and little bending of the knee or rising to *demi-pointe*. It is always danced *de face* to a supposed audience, or facing the centre of a circle.

11. Theatrical form of pas de basque. No. 1.

Commence 3rd position, hands on hips.
anacrusis. Raise well stretched R leg diagonally forwards 25°, opening R arm upwards and slightly turning body towards leg and circling R towards side with quick *fondu* L.

1. Spring off L transferring weight to R and bring L knee bent across to R. Body slightly turns towards right as L shoulder swings forwards.
and. Drop L foot in small 4th and without changing position of R foot raise R heel from floor. The weight of the body is thus transferred to L.
2. Bring R to L and with slight tap of R *demi-pointe* place it behind L.
and. Open L as on anacrusis above and repeat *pas de basque* to other side remembering to change the position of both arms and body.

The arms can also be held on hips or opened into 2nd when moving to the right and closed on hips when moving to the left.

12. Pas de Basque No. 2.

The *pas de basque* can also be danced with the smallest of springs from one foot to the other at the fastest tempo. The feet scarcely leave the floor. The body can lean very slightly backwards and thus does not fall in the direction taken by the feet, i.e. it is held *de face*. In this version the arms can be on the hips or opened into a low 2nd, they must never rise above shoulder level.

STUDIES IN RUSSIAN DANCE

13. Jumping from one foot to the other with slaps.
Commence normal position, arms opened sideways.
anacrusis. Raise R leg sideways with simultaneous *fondu* L.
1. Spring on to R raising L knee well bent to 90°, simultaneously sweeping R arm across to L shoulder and circling it downwards to slap L foot (L arm rises sideways as R sweeps across body). Head inclines over R shoulder.
2. Repeat above springing on to R foot. Repeat at least 8 times.

The legs must be raised as high as possible, the weight of the body being transferred easily from one foot to the other so that the dancer inclines smoothly and evenly as the supporting foot reaches the floor. The arms must open widely and move freely from the shoulders.

The step should be practised and amalgamated in several types of *enchainements* where it should be performed with Squatting steps.

SQUATTING STEPS.
These steps are the particular property of the male character dancer. They are therefore discussed in a single chapter although they have a place in the dances of many peoples. However they are most typical of Russian and Ukrainian dance and it is difficult to say which particular step belongs to one or the other country. The steps included here are the most typical and are thus the most useful to study.

There are two types of Squatting steps. Those which require preparations from a smooth, flowing full *plié* and those which require a sharp, clean *demi-plié*. All such preparations must first be practised at the barre because their performance demands that all the leg and back muscles must be felt correctly and the movement of the legs must be felt to move from the hip joints or joint through the centre of the knee, ankle and foot. It is also important first to practise all squatting steps *en place* before attempting those which travel.

When practising these steps for the first time away from the barre, it is usual for the boy to place his hands on his hips, fingers bent inwards so that the wrists are straight and only the knuckles of the hands are visible. (Note drawings.)

CHARACTER DANCE

PREPARATIONS FROM DEMI-PLIÉS

14. No. 1.
Commence 3rd position, L *devant,* dancer facing and holding barre with both hands.
anacrusis. Spring upwards from *quarter plié,* lifting R toe to level of L ankle (i.e. R knee slightly bent) then straighten R leg out sideways with body inclined towards left.

1. Land on L foot, placing R heel on floor.
and. Jump upwards bringing both feet together in 3rd position R *devant.*
2. Land in *quarter plié.*
   Repeat whole stretching L leg out sideways. The movement should be repeated at least 8 times. It is most important to keep the knees and ankles stretching and bending freely and correctly. The barre must not be used to take the dancer's weight at the height of the jump. The head must be held erect, the student never being allowed to glance downwards.

15. No. 2.
Commence in 3rd, L foot *devant,* dancer facing with both hands on barre.
anacrusis – 1. Prepare and place R heel on floor as in No. 1 above.
and. Jump upwards bringing R leg back to 3rd *devant,* land on it and lift L foot to level of R ankle.
2. Stretch L leg out sideways and place L heel on floor.
   Continue as above using alternate feet. Repeat movement at least 8 times and always complete exercise in 3rd position *quarter plié* before stretching knees.

16. No. 3.
The above two exercises should also be practised moving from 1st position and when mastered should be tried so that each time the feet are joined in 1st in the air, the heels are clicked together.

STUDIES IN RUSSIAN DANCE

17. No. 4.
The above three exercises should then be practised so that each time the dancer descends from the jump he bends his supporting leg out sideways to its fullest as he stretches the working leg out sideways with heel on the floor.

18. No. 5.
The most difficult form of the above is where the dancer has to move immediately through one single jump from one fully bent supporting leg to the other. It is essential to ensure that the student has completely mastered the first form of this exercise with a fully bent leg and a pause between the jumps before attempting Nos. 4 and 5.

19. No. 6. Demi-pliés springing on to the Heels.
Commence normal position, holding barre with both hands.
anacrusis. *Quarter plié*.
1. Slightly spring forwards on to both heels with fully stretched legs so that the weight of the body remains roughly over the original centre. The heels must be firmly anchored to the floor with toes upturned.
and. Spring lightly back to original place on *demi-pointes*, both knees bent.
2. Spring both legs fully stretched outwards into wide 2nd position and, as before, anchor both heels well into floor as toes are upturned.

Repeat by springing swiftly back into preparatory *quarter plié* as on anacrusis above.

Repeat 8 times in all.

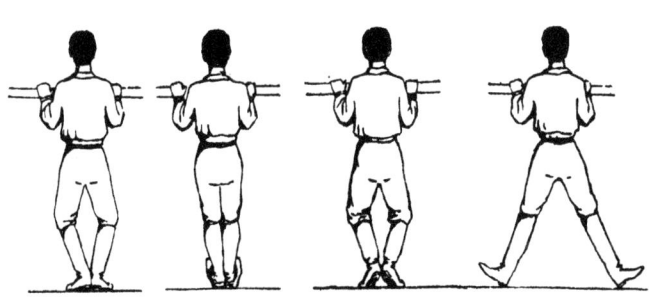

CHARACTER DANCE

20. No. 7.
Commence in 3rd R *devant*, facing and hold both hands on barre.
anacrusis. *Quarter plié*, spring upwards raising R leg knee bent until toe is level with and in front of L ankle.
1. Land on L *fondu*, resting R toe (knee still bent) in front of L toe.
2. With another small spring off L, stretch R leg put sideways and rest heel on floor, toe upturned. Turn head to left.
   Repeat movement on opposite side. Repeat at least 8 times in all.
   The legs throughout the above must be as turned-out as possible. It is essential to hold the weight firmly over the supporting leg as it lands *fondu*. It is also very important not to stub the working toe when it rests momentarily in 3rd position, and equally important not to rest any weight on the outstretched heel.

21. No. 8.
Repeat No. 7. springing from one foot to the other using the deepest possible *fondu* as the working leg is stretched out sideways on the heel.

22. No. 9.
The above should also be practised as follows: Repeat the first bar as in No. 7 above then:
1. Spring lightly upwards clipping both heels together briskly in the air before landing on L *fondu* and stretching R leg out sideways to 2nd position and tapping R heel on floor.
2. Repeat this movement landing on R foot and tapping L heel on floor.
   Repeat 8 times in all.

23. No. 10.
No. 9 must now be practised using the deepest possible *fondu* as the leg is stretched out sideways. However it is not advisable to increase the height of the preparatory spring upwards.

24. No. 11. Demi-plié and leg opening used in the centre.
Commence in normal position.
1. Deepest *plié* raising both heels from floor and hands on hips.
2. Spring slightly straight upwards simultaneously opening R leg out sideways fully stretched until the heel rests on floor, toe upwards.

Repeat 4 times in all with alternate feet. The arms can be used in many ways: both opened sideways with palm upwards; held across chest; one opened sideways on working side, the other thrown out sideways and upwards.

25. No. 12.
No. 11 is more theatrical if the leg is opened outwards into the air above 35°

with the toe turned upwards, or with the working leg well stretched well outwards with the toe resting on the floor.

26. No. 13. Demi-plié brushing the foot forwards on the heel.
Commence in normal position.
1. Full *plié*.
2. With a slight spring upwards simultaneously stretch R leg forwards placing heel either *croisé* or *éffacé*. L leg must be well turned-out *fondu*. Repeat using other foot and making a very deliberate change of *épaulement* after going through the central *plié*. The arms can be used as in No. 12 above and repeat no more than 8 times.

27. No. 14.
No. 13 should be practised stretching the working leg out sideways on the heel.

Repeat no more than 8 times.

28. No. 15. Demi-plié brushing the leg out sideways on toe and heel.
Commence in normal position.
1. Full *plié*.
and. Spring upwards turning R leg inwards, knee bent and placing toe on floor, body inclining sideways to right, R shoulder a little forwards as eyes glance at R foot.

2. Spring slightly on L in same place, opening R leg out sideways to rest R heel on floor and inclining body to left – L *fondu* and straighten head.
and. Pause.

Repeat with opposite foot. Repeat 8 times in all.

29. No. 16.

A more elaborate version of No. 15 is of particular use in Hungarian dance, but is seldom used in Russian dance. It is included here as it uses the same basic technique.

N.B. Time signature 4/4. Commence normal position.

anacrusis. Raise R leg *éffacé devant* to 25°.

1. With a slight spring drop to low *fondu* and centering weight over R foot simultaneously bend L knee so that it almost touches floor by R toe.
2. Raise R leg from bent position by springing on to it forwards and landing on whole foot simultaneously raising L and stretching it *croisé devant* to 45°.
3. Step on L foot so that R remains behind, both feet finishing 4th firmly on floor and turned outwards.
4. Bring R foot with a stamp behind L.

N.B. The last two movements must be practised until they can be performed in a single beat as it is important on stage to pause on fourth beat of bar.

30. No. 17. Demi-plié on to the toes.

Commence normal position.

1. Full *plié*.

2. Rise and turning both knees inwards spring lightly on to toes. Knees are slightly bent and appear as if joined together.

Repeat 8 times in all.

The main difficulty is to maintain balance when standing on the toes, knees turned inwards, it is therefore important to wear the correct type of boot, i.e. with very little heel and flexible soles.

31. No. 18.

The above exercise should also be practised very swiftly rising from the *demi-plié* on to the toes, knees bent inwards then turning the legs outwards to rest on the heels in 2nd position. Repeat 8 times.

32. No. 19. Demi-plié with changes from toe to heel.

Commence in normal position.

1. Full *plié* directing knees to right.

and. Slightly spring upwards taking weight on R *demi-pointe éffacé* with knee bent, L leg turned inwards with knee bent and toe resting on floor behind R heel.

2. Skid or slide R foot forwards fully on sole of foot until R leg is stretched in front of L and rests on heel. Body inclines backwards.
and. Pause.

Movement is immediately repeated on other side. The hands can be held on the hips throughout.

33. Travelling from Side to Side.

Commence normal position.

1. Quarter *plié* directing both knees to right and opening arms to 2nd.
and. With slight spring, enough to carry body forwards, rise on *pointes*.
2. Drop on R foot simultaneously brushing L foot forwards until L leg straightens and rests *croisé devant* on floor.
and. Pause.

CHARACTER DANCE

Repeat on other side.
N.B. The head is always turned away from direction travelled. Both Nos. 18 and 19 and 20 are always danced in a diagonal line when used on stage.

34. Demi-pliés with pauses on heels in 2nd or croisé positions.
Commence normal position.

Bar 1.
1. Full *plié* opening arms to 2nd.
2. Spring upwards simultaneously stretching L leg *croisé devant* until it rests on heel, R rests on *demi-pointe*, knee bent with body slightly inclined backwards although weight must be held firmly over both feet. Head turns slightly towards back foot.

Bar 2.
Repeat spring from *demi-plié* into 2nd position on heels.
   Repeat with other foot.

35. Demi-plié changing Feet during Jump.
Commence normal position.
1. Full *plié*.
2. Spring upwards opening feet to 4th *croisé* so that R leg rests on heel and L on toe, body inclined backwards over L (knee slightly bent).

Bar 2.
1. Spring upwards changing feet in air by strongly bending both knees and slightly twisting body.

2. Land with L *croisé devant* on heel and R on *demi-pointe*, knee bent.
   Repeat not more than 8 times.

The important aspect of this exercise is the change of feet in the air when the weight of the body must be absolutely centered at the height of the jump. This is only possible if the heels are pressed into the floor very strongly as the dancer springs upwards from the full *plié*. It is essential that both legs work equally and that the spine is erect but mobile to withstand any strain. The arms are held in 2nd.

SQUATTING MOVEMENTS.

The chief problem with all squatting steps is to ensure the strength and correct mobility of the spine, i.e. it must be absolutely controlled, the head held high, a straight line being seen to run from the crown of the head to the coccyx or tail. If it is not held correctly and a clear right angle made at the junction of body and hip, there can be no stability. Another important point to note is that when the dancer is in the lowest squatting position, both knees in front, the centre of the spine is directly above the heels (see sketch overleaf).

It is always best to practise these squatting steps firstly with one hand on the barre and only at the end of a lesson when the muscles are thoroughly warm. No more than two or at the most 3 exercises should be attempted. It is also important that they are only tried when a boy's muscles are seen to be strong and well-disciplined.

N.B. In the following exercises the time signature is 2/4 unless otherwise stated.

36. Preparatory exercise No. 1.

Commence normal position full *plié*, i.e. knees and toes directed straight forwards.

anacrusis. Raise body by slightly stretching knees, i.e. roughly rise to *demi-plié*.

1. Raising R knee a little push R *demi-pointe* straight forwards until R heel is level with tip of L toe. L *demi-pointe* and knee remain in place, but sink to what was full *plié*. Both knees must be directed forwards.

CHARACTER DANCE

2. Change feet as smoothly as possible. Continue changing feet using *quarter pointe*. Gradually increase the distance travelled by the working foot forwards: firstly to a distance where the sole rests momentarily on the floor; secondly until the working leg is fully stretched forwards and the heel rests momentarily on the floor before the feet are changed.

N.B. There is no spring in this exercise. It is essential that the knee movement is first practised at the barre, one hand holding for support as the stance gained there is possibly the most important preparation for any Russian Squatting steps and their variations.

37. Preparatory exercise No. 2.
Commence normal position, full *plié* as above.
1. Stretch R leg directly forwards until it rest on heel.
2. Bring it back to full *plié*.

Now repeat same with L foot and repeat no more than 8 times in all before rising. As above there is no spring as the working foot stretches forwards. The whole movement must be smooth and the body held erect and steady.

38. No. 3.
Once the above has been mastered a brief spring on the supporting leg should be introduced. It occurs simultaneously with the stretching forwards of the working leg. The spring must not push the body upwards. It should only be sufficient to allow the dancer to transfer weight from one foot to the other.

39. No. 4.
A further development of No. 3 occurs when the working leg is stretched forwards toe fully pointed, but raised to 90°, i.e. toe level with hip joint.

Repeat 8 times only.

In this version it is absolutely essential to keep the body fully erect, still and centrally balanced. Thus the muscles in pelvis and stomach must be fully controlled throughout the *enchainement*. It is also essential to direct the working leg straight forwards with NO suggestion of turn-out. Only thus can the stability of the pose be maintained.

N.B. In this form of Squatting, it is usual to fold the arms across the chest when the student works in the centre.

Once the preparatory exercises Nos. 3 and 4 for Cobbler's steps have been mastered the student should have no fear about any other Squatting step.

40. Squatting with the leg thrown sideways. No. 5.
Commence full *plié*.

1. With a slight spring on L throw R leg out sideways fully stretched until it rests on heel (i.e. toe is upturned).
2. With a slight spring on L, bring R back to L simultaneously throwing L leg out sideways as on first beat i.e. change weight as feet meet in full *plié*.

It is important that this step is performed as fast as possible in order to keep the body centrally balanced and erect during the change of feet. The arms should be held in 2nd and kept as level as possible.

41. Squatting with leg thrown backwards. No. 6.
Commence full *plié*.
1. With slight spring on L, simultaneously turn and bend R leg inwards so that the dancer is all but kneeling, toe resting behind the body. R knee should be level but resting under L knee. Body slightly inclines forwards.

2. With a slight spring on L, but without rising from floor, change position.
Repeat no more than 8 times. Arms are usually held folded across chest.

If students have difficulties performing this step, it is useful to bring the working leg back to full *plié* before stretching the other backwards. In this way they should be able to maintain an erect body and give stability to the movement.

42. Squatting, Lowering to the Knee and Opening to the Side. No. 7.
Commence full *plié*.

1. Slightly spring on L, turning leg outwards with knee bent and simultaneously bend R so that dancer is kneeling all but *éffacé* 1, lower half of leg resting with toe pointed behind body. R knee should be below L knee R. shoulder is very slightly turned to audience.

2. With slight spring on L and without rising from floor, fully stretch R leg out sideways until heel rests on floor.

Repeat other foot. Repeat no more than 8 times in all.

It is usual to place L hand behind the head and R hand on the hip when weight is over L leg on first beat. The arms are then thrown out into 2nd on second beat with body inclined slightly sideways over L leg, i.e. the supporting leg. They are then reversed.

43. Squatting Travelling Sideways. No. 8.
Commence full *plié*.

Bar 1.

1. After slight spring on L, keep knee bent and lower sole of foot to floor simultaneously stretching R leg out sideways to right on heel.
2. Again spring on L, travelling to left and holding R leg fully stretched with heel firmly held on floor.

Bar 2.

1. Repeat second beat as above.
2. With slight spring join feet in normal position full *plié*.

Repeat other side travelling to right. Repeat all no more than 4 times.

During the travelling movement impetus is not only given by the supporting foot, but also by the body, thus its upright position and strong hold of the shoulders are very important.

44. Squatting with Circling of the Leg. No. 9.
Commence full *plié*.

1. Slightly spring and turn-out L leg lowering heel to floor simultaneously circling R leg in front of L, bending knee as if it were about to circle under L knee.
2. Slightly spring on L returning R to full *plié*. (Both knees must be turned-out at this point.) After which spring on R and circle L as above.

Repeat no more than 4 times with each foot. The arms are usually folded over the chest.

45. A Variation of above. No. 10.
From a full *plié*, dancer springs twice on L before changing feet and pauses momentarily in full *plié* before repeating on opposite side.

Repeat 8 times only.

The greatest mistake in this step is to allow the student to move backwards during the spring as the feet close in full *plié*. When correctly performed the step should be danced *en place* and as fast as possible.

46. Squatting Brushing the Working Foot on the Knee of the Other Leg. No. 11.
Commence full *plié*.

1. Lightly spring and turn-out L leg simultaneously raising R, knee bent and rest R toe across and just above L knee (see sketch 100).
2. Spring from L to R foot, bringing L foot across R knee, i.e. reverse the movement through a single spring.

Repeat not more than 8 times.

47. Squatting and Slapping the Sole of the Foot. No. 12.

This is the most effective theatrical version of squatting steps. Commence full *plié*.

Bar 1.
1. After a slight spring on L, sharply stretch R forwards, toe upwards and to left; hold it momentarily in the air.
2. Spring lightly from L to R foot, stretching L leg forwards also to left (i.e. *croisé*).

Bar 2.
1. Spring on L as on first beat above.
2. Spring on R as above but simultaneously lift L leg, knee bent in the air and cross R arm over L shoulder before sweeping it downwards with a broad movement to slap inside of L foot with R palm, then open arm to side.

Repeat other side. Repeat no more than 4 times in all with each foot. This step is best used when amalgamated with other squatting steps.

48. Squatting and Thrusting the Leg forwards in the air. No. 13.

Commence full *plié*.
1. With slight spring upwards, thrust both legs straight forwards into the air and return to full *plié*.

Repeat above on second beat of bar. Repeat no more than 8 times.

This movement is best practised as part of an *enchainement* in the same style as No. 12. The body must be inclined slightly forwards from the hip joint, spine straight so that the weight is fully centred over the feet as they land in full *plié*.

49. Squatting, Thrusting the Leg out Sideways into the air. No. 14.

In this exercise the dancer springs higher than in No. 13 and stretches both legs sideways into the air first to one and then the other side. The body must be held more erect than in No. 13 and the weight must be more carefully centered when the feet return to full *plié*.

50. Polzounok. Semi Bell Step. No. 15. (In Ukrainian dance this is known as *Metelki.*)

Commence full *plié*.
1. Spring slightly forwards on L simultaneously turning R leg inwards and circling it in a half circle forwards from an *éffacé* half kneeling position to just in front of L toe. It is important that as the circling begins the lower leg, toe pointed faces and glides over the floor.

2. Having completed the half circle, bring R foot back to full *plié*, but this time the R foot is a little in front of L.

Repeat circling with L foot and no more than 8 to 16 times.

It is most important to keep the weight centered over the supporting leg as the working leg circles. The body must never be held stiffly, but slightly inclined from side to side. The legs must appear to glide over the floor very smoothly and swiftly, giving the impression of the swinging of a bell, the supporting leg appearing as the clapper. The arms should be stretched in 2nd, palms upmost.

51. Squatting known as Liagoushka. No. 16.

In this step it is essential to use the arms as strongly and accurately as they are used in athlete's training. There are many ways of performing *Liagoushka*, the following is the most usual.

Commence normal position.

Bar 1.
1. *Demi-plié.*
2. Spring upwards and outwards on to the heels in 2nd, arms fully stretched sideways.

Bar 2.
1. Full *plié*, knees well turned-out.
2. With another slight spring simultaneously stretch both legs out backwards and press body forwards so that it rests on fully stretched arms,

CHARACTER DANCE

hands placed firmly on the floor. The body should now be in a straight line from head to heels supported by the toes of both feet and arms. There should be no arching of the back and the arms are directly in front of their own shoulder.

Bar 3.
1. Spring legs back to *demi-plié*, straightening body and folding arms across chest.
2. Spring legs into 2nd on heels and open arms to side.

Bar 4.
It is usual to hold one bar before repeating movement.
   Repeat no more than 4 times.
   In Ukrainian dance the above is frequently performed as one movement in an *enchainement* very often after *Metelki* which also often includes or begins with a *pirouette* from a full *plié* and then stretching the body over the floor. This type of work is very difficult and needs great care and long practice.

52. Pirouette Rising from the Floor.
Commence normal position.
1. Prepare by moving R foot into 4th *croisé*, R knee half bent and L almost straight. R arm is across chest and L in 2nd, i.e. preparation for *pirouette en dedans*.
and. Swiftly bend R knee to lowest *fondu* simultaneously turning L leg inwards, knee bent until lower leg, toe stretched, is parallel to floor. N.B. L knee must be directly under R knee. From this position immediately rise into one or two *pirouettes*, straightening knees and thus lifting the body. Impetus for the *pirouette* must be taken from the L shoulder.
2. Complete *pirouette* by firmly placing R foot in 4th *derrière* with L hand on hip and R arm raised high to side.
and. Pause.

This movement should be practised on other side. The essential item in this step is the swift and direct bending and gradual stretching of the supporting leg and the student's ability to give impetus for the *pirouette* and raising of the body from the shoulder coming into the turn (as above the L shoulder when turning on the R leg or vice versa). In such steps the weight of the body must be directly over the supporting leg. The best results are also obtained if the student turns on a good *demi-pointe*.

53. Squatting Pirouette with Leg held forwards on Heel.
Commence normal position.
1. Commence as in No. 52 above.
and. Swiftly sink into deepest *fondu* on R and giving impetus from L shoulder simultaneously stretch L leg forwards (toe upwards) so that L knee is on a level with and pressed against R knee and complete one or two turns to right. N.B. L heel rests on floor.
2. Complete *pirouettes* in No. 52 above.

It is most important to study the taking of "Force" (impetus) from the shoulder coming into the turn without upsetting the balance of the body and without twisting the knee or ankle in any way once the turn has begun.

54. Squatting Pirouette Raising the Leg in the Air.
This is the same as No. 53, but the L leg is stretched fully forwards, toe upturned but held in the air, i.e. L knee is at same level as R knee.

This is the most difficult *pirouette* to perform because the weight of the body must be held firmly over the R leg whilst turning one or two *pirouettes* without the L leg slackening or dropping to the floor. It is also a preparation for the so-called *Melnitsy* (Mill-wheel).

55. Melnitsy or Mill-wheel.
Commence full *fondu*, R, heel off floor and L leg stretched fully forwards, heel resting on the floor, toe upturned. L knee must be just in front and close to R knee. Arms are stretched downwards, fingers resting on the floor. From this position the dancer spins himself round to right by using his hands one after the other to give impetus. The amount of turns performed and the tempo depend entirely on the context of the dance or the teacher's orders. The movement always ends with a slight spring to bring the feet together in full *plié*, then a stretching upwards to normal position, the arms opening sideways.

Another version of this type of *Melnitsy* can be performed with the L leg stretched backwards. The body must stretch forwards on to the fully stretched arms and the hands must be slightly turned out at the wrists, palms down. This enables them to propel the dancer round more easily.

It is essential to ensure that the arms not only take the weight of the body, but also move in absolutely strict tempo and rhythm if the turn is to gain speed.

STUDIES IN RUSSIAN DANCE

56. Volchok. Wolf Step.

Commence R leg in deepest *fondu*, heel raised from floor with L knee bent, toe pointed and resting on floor behind body which inclines forwards, resting on arms. Hands are slightly bent at wrists so that fingers can propel the dancer round at speed (as in No. 55).

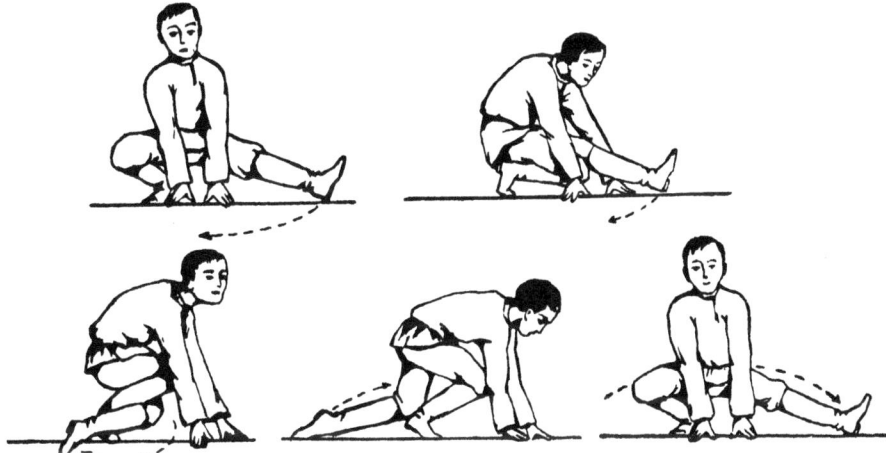

57. Melnitsy Jumping over the Working Leg.

Commence R leg in deepest *fondu*, L stretched outwards to side, heel resting on floor, toe upturned, arms stretched downwards, finger-tips resting on floor and body slightly inclined forwards.

anacrusis. Circle L leg towards R, when it is directly in front of R knee, bend it inwards simultaneously passing L hand over L leg and replacing finger-tips on floor. Bend L leg as far as possible towards R (L ankle should be level with R calf).

1. With a slight spring, jump R leg over L. Weight of body must be centered and held over both arms equally and will incline further forwards.
2. L leg continues circling but stretches backwards, toe stretched and facing floor, before returning to side on heel as on anacrusis.

Repeat movement no more than 4 times at beginning of practise. Later increase number and speed until at least 8 circlings can be made.

To complete step dancer usually springs straight upwards as working leg reaches side with arms outstretched into 2nd.

The most important element of this step is to ensure that the circling of the leg is as widely rounded as possible and the arms hardly seen to work at all because of the speed at which they perform.

2. Studies in Hungarian Dance

Although the characteristics of Hungarian dance are very obvious, those appearing in the old classical ballets are very much influenced by the techniques of A. Bekefi, the great character dancer, who performed at the Marinsky from 1883–1914 as well as with Diaghilev and then taught until his death. He was Hungarian by birth and his particular style was greatly envied and copied. It is those steps which were so associated with his dancing that are given here.

Any Hungarian dance in true folk style consists of two sections, the Lassan or slow followed by the Friss or fast. The tempo remains unaltered. It is either slow or fast.

It is essential to understand the use of the term "skid" in Hungarian dance. Translated literally it means "under-jump", i.e. the dancer hops slightly forwards with bent knee and travels on the whole foot without lifting the heel nor apparently raising the body to a higher level.

1. Promenade No. 1.
Time signature 4/4. Commence normal or 3rd position.
anacrusis. *Grand battement développé éffacé devant R*, slightly bending L knee.
1. Step R into 4th immediately transferring weight of body and raising L foot, toe full stretched just off the floor to side of R ankle.
2. Step L, knee slightly bent and *grand battement développé R*.
3. Repeat first beat.
4. Place R foot on floor knee fairly straight, simultaneously bending and then stretching L into *grand développé devant*.

STUDIES IN HUNGARIAN DANCE

This last movement begins the repeat of the step with L foot. The direction taken is very important. If it is to be straight forwards the dancer must change *épaulement* slightly on the first beat of each bar, i.e. first bar will be *éffacé* commencing R foot, second bar will be *croisé*. It can also be danced so that each bar is *éffacé*. In each case the body slightly inclines towards the raised leg, or the shoulders slightly turn towards it.

The promenade can be danced andante or allegro, but must never lose its look of controlled strength and precision.

Several *ports de bras* can be used, i.e. both hands held across the chest; one or the other arm opened sideways with first *développé*. When dancing with a partner boy places his R hand behind the girl's waist; if they are dancing face to face he places both hands on her waist and she places one hand on his shoulder.

2. Promenade No. 2. This is only danced to the Friss or quick music.
Time signature 2/4. Commence as in No. 1 above, but the *grand développé devant* only occurs on the first beat of the bar simultaneously with a *skid* forwards L, i.e. that form of hop in which the whole of the foot keeps contact with the floor, L knee slightly bent. This is followed by step R, close L to it, then small step forwards R.

3. Promenade No. 3 with clip. This is only danced to the Lassan, or slow section.
Time signature 4/4. Commence normal position.
anacrusis. Simultaneously spring on L turning body to left and stretching R leg forwards in air (N.B. to left the turn of the body sends the R leg out sideways. The spring of L, brings R to L clipping heels together *en l'air* with both legs fully stretched,
1. Land on L simultaneously raising and stretching R *battement développé devant* as body turns *de face*.
2. Step R.
3. Bring L to R.
4. Step R and turn body to right, stretching L forwards as on anacrusis above.
   Repeat other foot.

This step often begins a stage dance and is usually danced only to the Lassan. If genuine Hungarian folk music is used there should be a slight hold of the working leg as it is stretched outwards. The *clip* of the heels is also widely used in all theatrical versions of Hungarian dance.

4. Promenade No. 4.
Time signature 4/4. Commence with slight *skid* on L raising R, knee bent before straightening it. Open L arm to side and R above head, both elbows bent. Do not stretch fingers. Body inclines to left and slightly backwards. anacrusis. *Clip* R foot against L before L returns to floor and *clips* again against R (i.e. two tiny springs on L) then returns to floor and R is raised with knee bent.
1. Small *skid* forwards L simultaneously stretching R forwards from 80–90°, to upturned, R arm together with body slightly thrown backwards, L should be brought forwards and L arm crossed over chest, L hand on R shoulder.
2–3. 2 large steps forwards swinging arms across body.

4. Small step R as L with body and arms return to original starting position, ready to repeat from anacrusis above with L foot.

The *clip* must be light yet strongly marked. It should be heard as an accent to each fourth beat of the bar. The step should always be danced in a diagonal line, never *de face* to the audience.

5. Holubetz No. 1. (ordinary form. It is also known as Break No. 1.)
Such steps mean that one foot is *clipped* against the other and is distinguished from the more classical *cabriole* in that both legs take part equally and the legs are directly under the body. The weight of the body is usually transferred as both feet complete the *clip*. Unlike the true *cabriole* which is a jump from one foot to the same foot.
Time signature 2/4. Commence normal position.
1. Without lifting toes from the floor, twist both legs inwards, knees slightly bent and heels raised.
2. Twist legs outwards *clipping* and lowering heels before returning to original position.

6. Holubetz No. 1 with variation.
This must also be practised taking only half a beat for each movement. Thus there will be two *clips* to each bar, which should be as fast as possible.

A further development requires that the heels must be *clicked* twice before lowering the heels.

7. Holubetz No. 2. Brush and swing to the side.

Time signature 2/4. Commence normal position, L hand on hip, R arm bent at elbow and crossed front of waist, fingers just touching fingers of L hand.

anacrusis. Simultaneously bend L knee and swing R leg out sideways, toes on floor.

1. *Clip* heels together by bringing R towards L which also moves very slightly towards R. Heels must meet, dancer on quarter *pointe*.

and. Stamp R besides L, body *de face* and then slightly turned left.

2. Stamp L beside R.

and. Pause.

During beats 1 – and gradually lift R elbow bent to chest level. This *ports de bras* is very characteristic.

Repeat other side being careful to change arms.

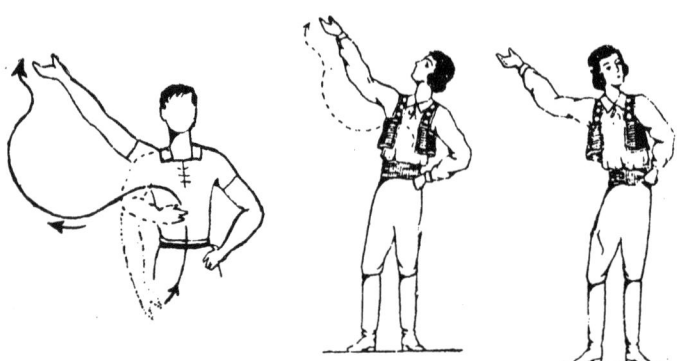

8. Holubetz No. 2 variation.

If the above Break finishes with a stamp R and is the end of an *enchainement*, then it is more usual to finish with the feet in a small 4th and the R arm uses another *ports de bras*, i.e. drop R arm from chest level to side, raise it through 1st before swinging it downwards slightly and then up to 2nd and 3rd with palm upwards. L arm remains on hip. The body turns very slightly to right and the head towards R arm, eyes looking into hand, or R shoulder can be taken backwards but head turned to left shoulder, which is brought forwards.

9. Holubetz No. 2. 2nd variation.
This is the same as No. 2 the dancer repeating the step but making a quarter turn, on 1st bar or twice to make a half turn to left. It is also possible to make a full turn with only one *holubetz*. In this case the two feet must move slightly apart and L in *fondu* during the *clip*.

The position of the arms when turning is all important, L hand is on hip, R across waist or opened to side, body held slightly backwards, head also turned backwards but to right. If the turn is danced with a partner, they must be face to face, L hips all but touching, boy holding L arm behind girl's waist and her L hand on his R shoulder (see sketch above).

10. Holubetz No. 2. 3rd variation.
A further development of above is where the dancers hold as above and as they stamp L foot (or R) they raise R leg, knee bent to 45° (see sketch above). R hands are placed behind their heads.

11. Bokso Liorka.
This movement is almost exclusive to Hungarian dance. Time signature 2/4. Commence normal position.

1. Small step forwards R immediately transferring weight of body. R knee slightly bent and directed forwards, L simultaneously stretches behind but toe does not leave floor. L knee bends and is brought forwards until it is almost level with R.

2. Drop L foot in normal position immediately transferring weight of body. Step is now repeated on other foot.

Hands are usually held on hips, finger forwards and thumbs behind waist. Weight of body must always be transferred directly onto supporting leg. Movement must be very controlled so that shoulders remain at same level.

12. Balancé Effacé. No. 1.
Times signature 2/4. Commence normal position.
anacrusis. Raise R leg sideways just off floor.
1. Simultaneously turn body to right and drop on R *fondu* with L knee bent and behind R ankle.
and. Join L to R, both on *demi-pointes*, knees slightly stretched.
2. Hop slightly R *en place*, raising L behind R ankle as before.

If the movement is to be repeated on L, then the leg must be swung out sideways as on anacrusis. The body must also turn *de face* before turning to left on first beat. The step can however be repeated on R.

The position of the arms, head and body is very important. On anacrusis head and body are in normal position, L arm bent at elbow, hand and fingers bent inwards and placed on hip. R arm is opened to side a little lower than shoulder level. On 1. Simultaneously turn body to right bringing L shoulder forwards. Body inclines to left and slightly backwards as does the head. R arm is raised, elbow bent and palm of hand behind back. (L arm does not move). On beats and – 2. Hold arm, body and head in position.

When repeating to other side, change arms.

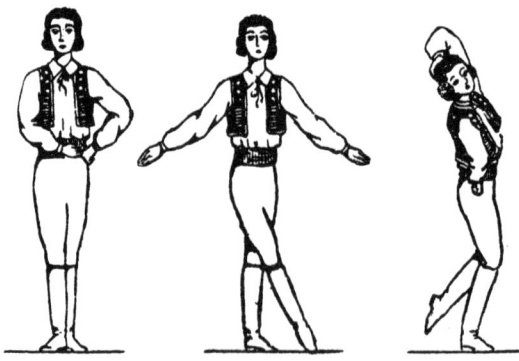

13. Balancé Croisé No. 2.
This is similar to No. 1. above, the difference being that the movement commences from 3rd position. R foot placed *croisé* in front of L and the body is turned to the left. (Sketch at bdottom of previous page.)

Balancé éffacé is usually danced slowly to Lassan and *balancé croisé* much faster to the Friss section.

14. Balance with Clip.
This *balancé* differs from the above as it involves a *clipping* of the heels and is called in Hungarian *Kiess Harang*, or *little bell step*.
Time signature 2/4. Commence normal position.
anacrusis. Without turning leg outwards, raise R sideways to 25° with *fondu* L, heel firmly pressed into floor.
1. Return R to normal position *clipping* it against and immediately raising L to side at 10° and lower L *demi-pointe* to take place of R. Both knees are all but fully stretched.
2. Slightly bend L knee whilst stamping R foot as it takes place of L, which swings out to side at 25°.
and. Pause.
   Repeat movement with other foot.
   On this step the arms are also very important. L hand is on hip and R arm opened to side on anacrusis. On 1. Lower R arm in front of body below waist. On 2. Bring R back to place on hip as L arm opens to side ready to repeat movement. On anacrusis body should incline to left and with opening of leg sideways on second beat, incline to right.
   It is important to keep the level of head and shoulders very steady as the body and legs swing from side to side. The legs should open as widely as possible, but not rise above 25°

15. Cabriole with Clip.
Time signature 2/4. Commence normal position. R hand on hip, L opened to side.
1. Small step L moving a little forwards to right (N.B. This step is made with short *skid*) opening R to side at 45°. R shoulder moves slightly forwards and body inclines slightly backwards to left as head turns *écarté* to right.
and. Spring off L, *clipping* heel against R in air and raising and stretching L arm a little higher. Shoulders, head and body must not change.

2. L foot returns to floor *fondu*.
and. Pause.
   Repeat movement with other foot.
   This step should first be practised at the barre. The position of the arms can be changed. Both can be held across the chest, or opened to the sides. The body also can be kept erect and a much higher spring be made to raise the leg to 90°. This version is called the *great bell step* and is often combined with the *little bell step* above. A typical *enchainement* is one *great bell*, 2 *little bells*, then 2 *great bells*.

16. Double Cabriole
This is performed as No. 15 above, but on second beat, return L to place then immediately step R across L, ready to repeat movement to opposite side without any pause.

17. Pas Tortillé. (Csapasolo.)
Time signature 2/4. Commence normal position.
1. *Skid* directly forwards R, swinging L forwards and upwards.
2. Again *skid* forwards R, swinging L backwards. Repeat 4 to 8 times and finish with a Break (see Nos. 24, 25, 26).

18. Verevochka. No. 1. (Hopping en place.)
Time signature 2/4. Commence normal or 3rd position R *devant*. L hand on hip, R opened to side with slightly bent elbow, L shoulder a little forwards and head slightly turned to left. (i.e. use classical *épaulement*).
anacrusis. *Skid* slightly forwards on L, knee bent and raise R, knee bent until heel of fully pointed toe is in front of and under L knee.

1. Place R *demi-pointe* on floor in place of L (it moves behind).
and. With another *skid* forwards R, raise L knee as on anacrusis.

Continue to repeat this movement 4, 8 or 16 times with alternate feet and dancing absolutely *en place*.

It is essential to keep the shoulders as still as possible as they slightly change *épaulement*. This movement must contrast to the sharp, accurate raising and lowering of the working leg. Arms can be held on the hips; opened to the side; across the chest; one on the hip and the other out to the side, and if applicable gradually raised upwards but without disturbing the shoulder line.

19. Verevochka No. 2. With a Turn.

This is the same as No. 1 but with the working foot always being placed behind in a small 4th or 5th position. The dancer turns to the right if the R foot begins in front, or Left if L in front.

It is usual to take 4 hops to a turn, although the expert soloist will only take 2 hops. And at the end of a series the arms must finish both firmly placed in the hips or opened to the sides.

20. Verevochka. No. 3. Moving Backwards.

Time signature 2/4. Commence in 3rd. R *derrière*.

This is similar to No. 1. but on anacrusis L *skids* backwards and R, knee bent is raised in front of L knee.

If turned the dancer moves to the right.

21. Walk with Fully stretched Leg.

Time signature 2/4. Commence normal position.
1. Step forwards R *fondu éffacé* and without moving L leg, raise L heel.
and. Bring L towards R and raise it *croisé devant* to 25° with fully stretched knee and foot. R must not change position.
2. Place L foot on floor immediately transferring weight of body and drop R to floor behind L.
and. Simultaneously and with turn of body to left, stamp R behind L, immediately opening L *éffacé*, ready to repeat other side.

It is possible to make a double beat on the heel of the supporting leg on last half beat of bar.

22. Lejtovagas. Lunge.

The preparatory form of the Hungarian lunge has already been given in barre-work (see *Grands Battements* No. 2). When danced on the stage these become more complicated.
Time signature 4/4. Commence normal position.
anacrusis. With hands on hips throw L leg forwards and sideways simultaneously opening L arm.
1. Spring on to L foot (*jeté porté*) sinking into deepest *fondu* simultaneously bring R on to floor, knee bent downwards and straight forwards until R

knee is under L. Body inclines very slightly backwards. Place L hand behind head which turns towards right.

2. Spring upwards simultaneously stretching R forwards and sideways to 25° ready to repeat other side. Or if preferred stretch R leg forwards to 90° simultaneously *skidding* forwards on L. Place R on floor and walk 2 steps forwards turning *de face* on second step and opening L leg as on anacrusis above ready to repeat other side.

The dancer can also take a large spring into the lunge in which case the working leg should not touch the floor as it passes from back to front, but should bend more strongly and be simultaneously stretched forwards as the dancer rises.

23. Step with Hand Clap. A step used to finish an *enchainement* which is to be repeated.
Time signature 2/4.
1. Stamp R 4th *croisé devant* bringing R shoulder forwards, knees slightly bent, R arm having opened to side is circled round to clap L hand from above, above waist level. Body slightly inclines forwards.
and. Stamp L behind R, straightening body.
2. Repeat stamp R, turning head to right and inclining slightly backwards, simultaneously opening R arm sideways and upwards as head turns to right. L opens sideways.
and. Hold.

A variation can be made by changing movement of body on second beat, i.e. incline backwards and look into L arm. Sketch a.

Another variation used more particularly when dancing with a partner is to raise R arm leaning slightly backwards on second beat whilst opening L arm, palm upwards towards partner. Sketch b.

24. Ordinary Break. Bokazo.
This break should first be practised at the barre to gain the necessary control and co-ordination of legs and arms.
Time signature 2/4. Commence normal position. R hand on hip, L hanging at side.
anacrusis. Small *demi-plié*.
1. Slight spring L simultaneously crossing R, knee bent, toe pointed in 4th *devant*. Both knees must be turned out with body and head inclined to left.
and. Bringing R foot back to L, raise heels from floor turning inwards and straightening body and head.
2. Join heels together with *clip* as used elsewhere and open R arm sideways and upwards, just above shoulder level.
and. Pause. Holding position on *demi-pointes*.

When this Break is danced in the centre, both hands on are hips then L is opened diagonally forwards at waist level on second beat.

25. Bokazo. No. 2. Double Break.
This is similar to No. 25 above.
Commence as on anacrusis and first beat above.
and. Slight spring on R before lowering whole R foot on floor and turning R knee inwards, L works as above, head and body inclined to right.
2. Repeat *clip* etc. as above.

26. A more Elaborate Bokazo. Break No. 3.
This should first be practised at the barre. R hand on hip.
Time signature 2/4. Commence normal position.
anacrusis. *Demi-plié* and spring in air.
1. Land on L *fondu*, crossing R, knee bent, toe pointed across in front of L.
and. Spring off L landing on R *fondu*, L knee bent, toe pointed in front of R before turning knees inwards by rising to *demi-pointes*.
2. Turn knees outwards, *clip* heels together before lowering them to floor.
and. Hold position, opening R arm upwards and sideways. Arms, head and body move as in No. 24.

27. Saut de Basque.

This step is often used to end a long phrase of *Verevochka*. No. 18.
Time signature 4/4 (for practice only).

It is supposed that the step commences on last beat of bar, dancer is on L *fondu*, R knee bent, toe resting in front of L ankle, weight of body directly over L foot, hands on hips.

1. Take short step R to right opening arms sideways simultaneously turning to right (thus nearly back to audience) and throw L leg upwards to 90°, when body is absolutely back to audience.

and. Circle L leg round as arms are raised above shoulder level.

2. Land on L *fondu* bringing R, as noted above and closing hands on hips.
3. Stamp R foot on floor 4th *devant*.
4. Hold position.

3. Studies in Polish Dance

The elements of Polish Dance as used in the late nineteenth century ballets were greatly influenced by the famous character dancer Kshessinsky, whose brilliant performances inspired so many artists and audiences. The importance of his work was to insist on the exact timing and phrasing of the various steps thus ensuring that the dancers preserved most of the characteristics exclusive to Polish folk dance. The two most typical of these used on the stage are the Mazurka and Krakoviak. The Obertass also makes an occasional appearance.

1. Girl's Pas Marché or sometimes called Pas de Basque.
This only differs from the classical form in that the dancer does not make a circling movement with the first step.
Time signature 3/4. Commence 3rd position, R *devant*.
1. Take small spring R, slightly forwards and simultaneously extend L forwards.
2. Step L with slight accent immediately transferring weight, stretching R and pointing toe straight forwards.
3. Step R allowing movement to travel from toe to heel before transferring weight.

To interpret this *pas marché* correctly the dancer must always allow the toe to reach the floor first, particularly on the third beat. Although the body appears to incline slightly backwards, this is due to the dancer's very erect carriage and ability to travel forwards in a sweep. The step must be very light and smooth. The girl's L hand rests on her partner's R hand and he guides her with the strength of his forearm. Her R hand can hold her skirt, or open easily to the side.

This step is little more than an easy run with a particular accent.

2. Boy's Pas Marché or Pas de Basque.
This differs from the girl's version in that he must mark the steps more strongly, particularly the second beat and hesitate slightly on the third beat before stepping on to R and then quickly bring L, knee bent and toes stretched beside R ankle (*coupé*) as well as *clipping* it against heel.

The weight of the body must be transferred directly on to the leading foot as it stretches on to the floor. It also inclines very slightly away from the girl. The boy's arms must be very controlled and strong. They are almost straight, palm upwards, particularly when holding the girl's hand. They are just below shoulder level. The L arm is often held slightly forwards as if showing the way: or the hand can be held on the hip, or more rarely and only when dancing with a partner, behind the waist.

N.B. It is very important that when dancing in opera such as *Eugene Onegin* (i.e. ballroom scenes) the girl must work on *demi-pointes* in contrast to the slightly heavier boy's run on the whole foot.

3. Balancé in Mazurka or Light Run.
Time signature 3/4. Commence 3rd position. R *devant*.
1. *Skid* on whole foot R and accent this well.
2. Short step on to L *demi-pointe* as in any classical *balancé*.
3. An energetic slightly accented step on whole foot. The body should incline gently from one side to the other, L arm is usually on hip and R usually held out sideways.

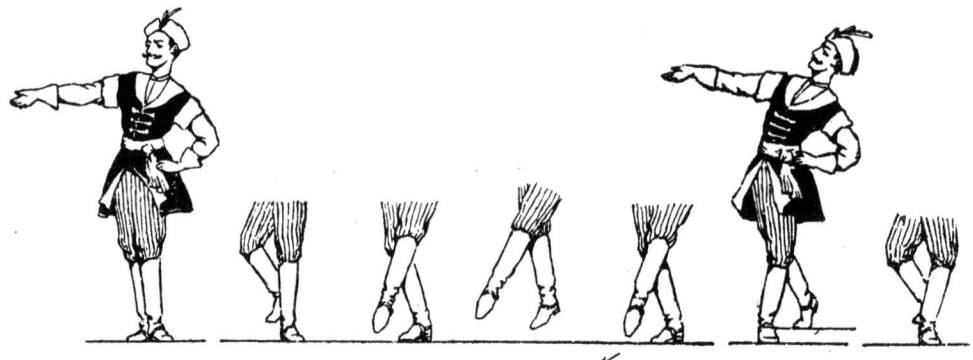

4. Pas-chassé coupé for Boys.
Time signature 3/4. Commence 3rd, L *devant*.
anacrusis. Stamp R, simultaneously stretching L fully forwards and immediately lightly *skid* on R *en place*. L must be held strongly.
1. Small step forwards L, allowing movement to travel through from toe to heel immediately transferring weight of body and lifting R foot.
2. Small *fondu* L and bending R knee, bring heel behind L.
3. Repeat movement of anacrusis above using same foot.

This variant of *pas marché* (i.e. Mazurka on one foot) is used by the boys only.

5. Basic Step of Mazurka for purely Character Ballets. i.e. Coppélia.
Time signature 3/4. Commence normal position.
anacrusis. Commence as 4 above but do not stamp so strongly.
1. Repeat first beat of No. 4. but lower L foot sharply and directly to floor.
2. Raise R knee bent and stretch it past L simultaneously *skidding* forwards on L so that –
3. Again *skid* forwards L, firmly holding position with knee slightly bent, R leg fully stretched forwards.

Repeat using other foot.

The body must be lifted upwards. The dancer travels onwards from the impetus given by the *skid* along the floor and the ability to control the depth of the *fondu*.

This step is one of the most difficult to control. The teacher must insist on the student's control and power over the space to be covered. The style is all important as the timing is very subtle. The *skid* occurs on the first quarter beat and the position is then held with the outstretched leg.

6. Holubetz with Partner in Mazurka.
Time signature 3/4. Commence normal position. R hand on hip, L crossed over body just below waist.
anacrusis. Stamp R sideways, L slightly bent and simultaneously twist L inwards without bending R knee, so that L rests on *demi-pointes,* also incline body slightly to right and move L arm sideways.
1. *Skid* R foot inwards to L and *clip* R heel against L, simultaneously turning L leg outwards.
2. Lightly bending L knee stamp, stepping slightly sideways to left and bring R foot to rest against L ankle.
3. Stamp R besides L.

CHARACTER DANCE

If it is necessary to repeat step then as R foot stamps on floor L must be raised sideways as on anacrusis.

During first beat R arm should move freely across the front of the body.

The most important aspect of this step is to *hear the clip* of one foot against the other on the first beat. It is important to remember that it occurs on the side of the heels as the legs must not be turned-out. It is also important to maintain the correct stance, *ports de bras* (see sketch above), body, shoulders and head held correctly but moving easily.

If an *enchainement* consists of three of these *holubetz* in one bar the dancer should conclude the phrase with *balancé*.

7. Another version of Holubetz. This is usually danced in court scenes, e.g. Act III, *Swan-Lake. Mazurka.*
Time signature 3/4. Commence as in No. 6. above. Hands on hips. anacrusis. as No. 6 above.

Bar 1.
1. Stamp L, raising R behind L ankle, knee bent and toe pointed inclining body to left.
2. Lower R *demi-pointe* behind L simultaneously raising L to level of R ankle, body still inclined to left.
3. Drop on L and swing R sideways to 25°.

Bar 2.
1. Spring into air bringing R to L *clipping* heels together with fully stretched legs before landing on R slightly *fondu* and body inclined to R.
3. Stamp R straightening body.
4. Stamp L.
   Repeat on opposite side.

8. Holubetz in the Krakoviak.
Time signature 2/4, commence standing half turned to audience, R shoulder forwards with head front, L hand on hip, R across body at waist level.
anacrusis. Stamp R, leg fully stretched (L also stretched).
1. Step R simultaneously turning body to right so that L shoulder comes towards audience with L knee bent, toes on floor facing right. As body turns, R arm opens sideways to shoulder level, head turns over L shoulder and body inclines slightly right.
and. With knee bent, place L in 2nd position. (R still stretched.)
2. *Clip* R heel against L.
and. Repeat as anacrusis above, but commencing L foot.

9. Another version
If using music by Glinka and other composers whose music does not start on anacrusis, then the double stamp on R occurs on first beat of bar and *Clip* on second beat.

10. Balancé Holubetz in Krakoviak. No. 1.
Time signature 2/4. Commence normal position, arms opened to side; crossed over chest; or on hips.
anacrusis. *Fondu* L simultaneously tapping R foot and immediately open sideways with toe on floor. Body inclines to left, head turns to right.
1. Stretch L knee returning R to normal position after *clipping* it against L, which moves sideways toe on floor as on anacrusis above.
2. Repeat movement on opposite side.

11. Balancé Holubetz in Krakoviak No. 2.
Time signature 2/4. Commence Normal position, body slightly turned with R shoulder to audience and hand on hip, L arm is held sideways a little higher than shoulder. Arms can also be held across chest or hands on hips. Head turned right. It is important to change position of arms during this movement.

anacrusis. *Fondu* L, stretching R sideways, toe on floor, incline body slightly left.
1. Bring R to L, *clipping* heels together and moving slightly backwards to left. Do not part heels as weight of body must be held above both legs equally. During *clip*, knees straighten and body inclines to right. After *clip*, raise R heel slightly.
and. Step R forwards to right, L remains in place with heel raised.
2. Place L behind R, inclining body to left.
and. Repeat on other side.

12.
A further variation of above is to combine it with No. 26, i.e. break of Hungarian dance which is danced turning and on the fourth bar complete the sequence with a clear stamp L to be ready to repeat on other side.

13. Legavey in Krakoviak.
Time signature 2/4. Commence normal position. R hand on hip, L opened sideways a little higher than shoulder, palm upwards. Head turned to right.

Bar. 1.
1. Stamp L, knee slightly bent, lifting R knee bent forwards, toe level with L ankle.
2. Straighten L knee and brush toe on floor across R to right and immediately transferring weight on to L although body inclines left.

Bar 2.
1. Stamp R foot normal position and bending L knee, brush L leg back to original position, immediately taking weight of body and raising R foot from floor.
2. Stamp R and place L hand on hip.
   Repeat on other side, being careful to reverse movements of body, head and arms.

14. Obertass Folk Dance. Entrance.

This dance consists mostly of the so-called Light Run i.e. No. 3 and little else but turning steps for the couple. These are usually phrased in series of 4 bars, e.g. the dancers commence with basic step, for 4 bars, and then some 4 bars of some figure.

e.g. Boy enters with R arm behind girl's waist and hers behind his. She holds her skirt with R hand and his L hand is behind his waist. The couple then change hands for the first figure. Boy faces girl and places his R hand in front of her waist and she places her R hand on his L shoulder. He does not usually move his L hand, but he can hold it slightly backwards. The above hold is absolutely characteristic of the Obertass.

First Figure.

First bar. Boy *fondu* L as far as possible, lifting heel from ground and stretch R forwards *éffacé* on to heel. Duing this bar, girl hops over boy's outstretched foot, helping herself by pressing her R hand on his L shoulder and her L hand on his R. This is called the *Obertass* or *Turn*.
second bar. couple repeat *Light Run* turning together.
Third and Fourth Bar. Repeat first 2 bars before returning to original hold.

Second Figure.

The above is usually considered too simple for the stage but is used in court scenes. A more elaborate version is however more usual.
Time signature 3/4. Commence on last beat of a four bar sequence, *demi-plié*. The boy only dances this. Girl runs round him or round stage.
1. Boy opens L leg sideways before swinging it forwards and placing whole foot on floor and kneel on R (toes on floor). Body is slightly turned with R shoulder forwards.
2. Pause.
3. Slightly spring upwards on L with slight turn, R held with knee bent and toe level with L ankle. Weight of body must be on L, R shoulder slightly turned towards audience, head inclined back.

Bar 2.
1. Complete turn with stamp R in front of L, now raised with foot parallel to floor and behind R ankle. Body *de face* weight over R foot, head turned and inclined right.
2. Stamp L straightening body and lifting R knee bent in front of L ankle.
3. Stamp R in normal position.

Repeat this figure making an 8 bar phrase in all.

During this step – N.B. boys only – he holds his R arm as if holding the girl's waist and guiding her (if she elects to dance round him). They should all but face each other.

Third Figure. Only danced by boy. The girl running round him as above. Commence on last beat of fourth bar with *demi-plié*.
1. Turn to right side lunging on L and stretching R directly behind body, toe pointed.
2. Pause.
3. Stretch upwards making half turn to right finishing with weight on L, slightly *fondu*, R stretched forwards on heel, body and head slightly inclined backwards.

During second bar complete turn by taking girl's waist and run with her.

4. Studies in Gipsy Dance

When studying Gipsy Dance it must be emphasized that it is always influenced by the dances of the country in which they travel or make their home. Therefore they always display the characteristics of another style of some native folk dance. However they have certain particular movements of their own and it is these that choreographers should show on the stage. These are to be found in older ballets created by choreographers closer to these "Travellers", than those of the twentieth century. Bournonville, Petipa, Saint-Léon and others studied the gipsy dances in many countries, particularly in Spain, Hungary and Romania.

The most prominent features of Gipsy Dance are firstly: Its apparent spontaneity. They dance extempore, when moved to do so by the music, a mood which they wish to convey to the audience. Secondly by the particular way in which the women ripple the upper parts of their bodies and arms by shaking their shoulders and breasts. This involved movement must be danced from the shoulders to the finger-tips. Thirdly the flexibility of their bodies, superb carriage and free movement of their heads. Fourthly the controlled, strongly rhythmic accents of the *clippings* and stampings of the men's feet. These accents must be heard.

1. Exercise for the Body Practised first at the Barre.
Time signature 6/8 andantino. Commence normal position, L hand on barre, R arm above head.

Bar 1.
Pressing both knees lightly together, full *plié*, curving head and body forwards and inwards until wrist is level with knees, hand bent downwards to floor.

Bar 2.
Straighten knees, stretch body and head upwards, raising arm above head. Then on last 3 beats, curve body backwards as far as possible.

Bar 3.
(1.2.3) Straighten body as before (4.5.6) then downwards and forwards as in Bar 1.

Bar 4.
Repeat Bar 2.

CHARACTER DANCE

Bar 5.
(1.2) Stretch upwards then immediately bend knees and curve body, head and arm downwards as before. (3) straighten knees and stretch upwards. (4.5.6) Bend backwards as before.

Bars 6 – 7 – 8.
Repeat 5th bar three times.

Repeat once only. The exercise must be timed very carefully, a slow, flowing tempo must be maintained throughout.

2. Basic Walk. (Theatrical interpretation.) This is like many other walks.
Time signature 2/4. Commence normal position.
anacrusis. Simultaneously step L stretching R forwards along floor and open R arm sideways bending L arm across body at waist level. Body and head slightly inclined and turned to right.
1. Step R allowing movement to travel through foot from toe to heel and as weight is transferred start raising arms a little.
and. Bring L *demi-pointe* behind R and transfer weight.
2. Small step R with slight stamp simultaneously bending L knee and bringing it towards R. Swing arms freely downwards and out to opposite side as head and body incline slightly to left.
and. Stretch L foot in front of R ready to step forwards on first beat of next bar.
   Repeat using L foot.
   The weight of the body must always be directly over the supporting leg as soon as its heel reaches the floor. This walk must always be directly forwards, the body alone swaying slightly from side to side with the movement of the arms, which must be strong yet expressive in boys and flowing for girls. The arms actually make a figure of eight (see p. 103).

3.
The same walk should be practised moving backwards. In this case the body and head do not incline or turn, as the dancer must appear to move straight backwards. The arms alone continue to move freely and the stamp on the second beat must not be so heavy.

STUDIES IN GIPSY DANCE

4. Saut de Basque.

This step is very typical of Hungarian Dance (see No. 11 Russian dance which is also used in Hungarian Dance) and is frequently used by Gipsies.

The dancers raise their arms and with elbows bent, clasp their hands behind their heads. The jump is not too high because they use a deeper *fondu*.

5.

In addition to the *Verevochka, Holubetz, Cabriole* and *Balancé* of Hungarian dance which are performed by the Gipsies with greater freedom of body movement and altogether more emphatic *ports de bras* a number of steps are used in which hands are clapped or slapped on each other or on the sides of the thighs, body and boots.

Time signature 2/4. Commence normal position.

1. Jump into 2nd *demi-plié* opening arms to side and inclining head and body slightly to right.

2. Hop R raising L, knee bent behind and slap L boot with R hand raising L arm over head.
Repeat picking up R foot and slapping it with L hand.

6.
Another basic movement is similar to Nos. 3 and 4 (i.e. Russian dance) the difference being that the feet are raised a little higher from the floor. If using No 4, the girl lifts her R hand to cheek level, whilst keeping her L arm bent and resting the wrist against her waist.

7. Holubetz with Clip No. 1. Boys only.
Time signature 2/4. Commence normal position, arms opened not too high sideways, body slightly turned right, shoulder forwards.
anacrusis. Simultaneously *fondu* L swinging R not turned-out sideways and with slight *skid* L, bring R to L *clipping* heels together. This sends L slightly backwards and sideways with knee bent before landing on R *demi-pointe*. Body inclines slightly forwards throughout. Arms are sideways as R leg moves and then inwards, L in front of waist and R down during change of feet.
1. Lower L toe with strong beat on floor and slapping L thigh with L hand.
and. Lower R heel transferring weight fully and raising L leg.
2. Stamp L close to R, which send R leg sideways as on anacrusis above. Open arms sideways.
Repeat as above.

STUDIES IN GIPSY DANCE

This step must be performed with an easy, clean beat as legs swing from side to side, body always inclined forwards. The arms swing in and out with the legs. Audience should hear five distinct beats. 1 *clip* 3 stamps or taps and the slap of the hand on the thigh. These sounds, especially the first, must be very precise and follow each other without pause. Always practise very slowly during the first attempts.

8. Holubetz with Clip. No. 2. Boys only.
Time signature 2/4. Commence normal position.
1. Stamp R *demi-pointe* moving slightly right, knee not bent but held freely and bending L knee.
and. Simultaneously slightly *skid* R back to original position marking beat against L toe, then immediately raise L, knee bent, but without opening it to side.
2. Lower L beside R, marking beat by rising on both *demi-pointes*.
and. Stamp L.
   Repeat commencing L foot.
   This *Holubetz* can also be danced with a clap of both hands in the air or a slap on the thighs on beats 1 or 2, or on both.

9. The Walk. Chetchetkoi. Girls only.
Time signature 2/4. Commence normal position.
anacrusis. *Skid* slightly L *demi-pointe,* dropping heel on floor whilst raising R, knee bent to level of L ankle.
1. *Flic-Flac* (see No. 9 barre-work) R foot transferring weight of body.
and. Bring L *demi-pointe* behind R.

2. Lightly lift then lower R *demi-pointe* with accent in front of L.
and. Repeat from anacrusis on other foot.

During this step the heels should not be lowered to the floor. The weight of the body is carried directly above the legs and is erect, but turns very slightly towards the raised foot on the anacrusis and to the other side with the *flic-flac*. At the beginning the L arm is usually held sideways, elbow slightly bent and R, with elbow bent roughly at head level.

10. Women's Walk.
time signature 2/4. Commence normal position. R arm with elbow bent raised to side, hand at head level, palm open to audience, L arm bent at elbow across body with palm open. Finger-tips are level with R upper arm. Head and shoulders incline slightly forwards.
1. Without changing body, small step forwards R *demi-pointe* in front of L (i.e. *croisé*), L rises to *demi-pointe* as weight is transferred.
and. Drop R heel, but do not stretch knee whilst passing L forwards and close to R. (Both knees must face forwards.)
2. and. Repeat movement with L foot.

This walk can be danced in a circle or diagonal line, but once its direction commences it must not change. The L hand (or R according to the direction taken) gradually lowers into the direction travelled and then raised again to the original position. The palm of the hand moves to face the floor. The R arm (or L see above) never changes position. The head is always inclined towards direction travelled with eyes glancing down.

11. Chetchetka. Boys only.

Time signature 2/4. Commence normal position.

anacrusis. *Flic-flac* R finishing R foot bent behind L ankle.

1. *Skid* slightly forwards L.

and. Beat R *demi-pointe* behind L, but do not transfer weight or straighten L knee.

2. Stamp R foot strongly raising L knee bent to level of L ankle.

and. *Flic-flac* L and repeat whole using L foot.

The dancer usually accompanies himself in this step by slapping his thighs or his body. The arms can also be held behind or at the sides of his body. Do not turn the legs out further than necessary.

Earlier it was stated that one of the most particular features of gipsy dance was the delicate way the women have of shaking the upper part of their bodies. The sketch below indicates the way in which the shoulders and arms are gently thrust forwards and backwards.

5. Studies in Spanish Dance

There are basically two types of Spanish dance used on the stage. Firstly there is the so-called classical dance which was so greatly influenced by French dancing-masters fleeing from the French Revolution of 1789 and later the Napoleonic Wars. They opened dancing schools which were attended by aristocratic families. Secondly there is Flamenco, or gipsy dance, which is displayed in the theatre as a high passionate, free-moving extempore performance. It became highly popular, but has now lost much of its spontaneity except in the hands of certain artists of the Kirov and Bolshoi companies who have been inspired to dance with and do as the gipsies.

The most popular Spanish dances staged theatrically are: 1. Bolero – 3/4. 2. Petenera – 3/8; 3. Panderos – 3/4; 4. Malguena – 3/4; 5. Sevillana – 3/4; 6. Jota Aragonesa – 3/8. These dances are set and never improvised. All their steps and poses are known and can be studied with Spanish dancing-masters. Castanets are used in nearly all of them. Another prominent feature is the Zapateado, or foot-work in which complex dance rhythms are beaten out by tapping and stamping toes, heel and the whole foot on the floor, thus giving various tones to the sound.

STUDIES IN SPANISH DANCE

The examples of steps given here are mostly from the works of Petipa, Gorsky and Bournonville (19th century choreographers) and Fokine from his *Jota Aragonesa*.

In teaching Spanish dance it is essential to obtain the correct stance and the controlled yet expressive movement of the head, body and arms as well as the precise foot-work, which must be practised *en place, en tournant* as well as travelling.

1. Preliminary Exercise for Foot-work. No. 1.

Time signature 2/4. Commence normal position. Head and body very erect, knees slightly bent, weight centered, although it appears to be more over heels. Therefore knees are just in front of body throughout.
anacrusis. Raise R foot to level of L ankle, knee directed forwards.
1. Tap *demi-pointe* stretching knee and transferring weight, lift L.
2. Tap L heel moving forwards as far as centre of R foot – R remains on *demi-pointes*, knee still slightly bent.
3. Repeat movement with L. i.e. reverse foot to tap floor with *demi-pointe*.

Continue step for at least 4 bars. The tap of the heel and then toe must be clear and brief as it is one of the basic steps of the Zapateado and when done correctly, develops into the easy, quick run with tiny steps, which covers much space although the feet are kept very close together. Correct stance must be maintained throughout.

2. Basic Foot-work. No. 2.

Time signature 3/4. Commence as above.

Bar 1.
Repeat movement of No. 1 three times, i.e. on R. L. R. feet.

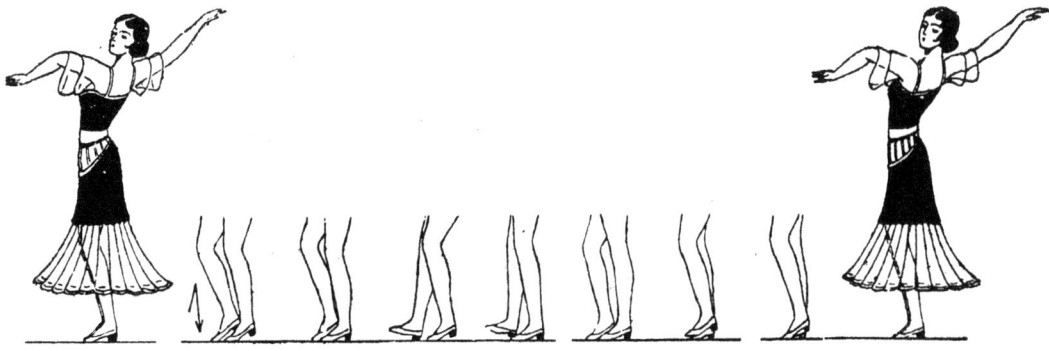

Bar 2.
1. Place L foot forwards, knee slightly bent and raise R heel *en place*.
2. Tap R *demi-pointe*, knee bent but not so far forwards as L.
3. Lightly stamp L without stretching knee. R does not move.
   Repeat commencing L foot.

This step should be practised in a diagonal line across the stage so that it is seen in profile. Sketch 199 suggests various *ports de bras* to be used and carefully note the difference between those for boys and those for girls.

3. Exercise for Foot-work. No. 3.
Time signature 3/4. Commence as above.
1. Tap R *demi-pointe* without bending knee and raising L foot; stamp L without moving R; beat R heel raising L heel; beat L heel just in front of R (i.e. 4 movements to this beat).
2. Tap R *demi-pointe*, lower and beat R heel (i.e. 2 movements to this beat).
3. Tap L *demi-pointe* then lower L heel with beat (i.e. 2 movements to this beat).

Repeat commencing same foot. The beat must be very clearly marked.

If this step is to be repeated 4 times, then the first movement on the first beat of the third beat should be the lowering of the L heel with a clear stamp and the step repeated commencing L foot.

The feet must work close to each other and never more than half a foot's length forwards or backwards. The beats on the *demi-pointes* must be very energetic but never heavy. The step should first be practised slowly and then speeded up.

4. Exercise for Foot-work. No. 4.
This is similar to the above, but after the first beat on *demi-pointe*, the rest of the step consists of very sharp beats on the heels alone, the body being kept absolutely still.

5. Beating (the Drob of Russian dance). Boy's step from Fokine's *Jota Aragonesa*.
Time signature 3/8. Commence normal position. (N.B. Beat in this step means that the whole foot is lightly stamped. Body is straight, L shoulder brought forwards with L arm, elbow bent, across waist in front. R also bent behind waist.)
anacrusis. Beat R sharply *en place*.

Bar 1.
1. Sharply stamp 3 beats *en place* – L.R.L.
2. Raise R *croisé devant*, beating heel on floor as it travels and gradually pushes away from L, which gradually bends.
3. Place R on floor very slightly backwards, beating L *demi-pointe* with knee stretched.

N.B. On second beat incline body slightly backwards and then straighten it on third beat.

Bar 2.
1. Take half step forwards by swinging L slightly forwards and then backwards before placing it on floor.
2. Raise R swinging it forwards and beating it on floor as it passes L. Be sure to hold weight of body over L as R shoulder swings backwards.
3. Place R, knee straight, firmly on floor.

   N.B. On first beat of this bar bring R shoulder forwards without changing arms and on second beat bring L shoulder forwards.

Bar 3.
1. Raise L and swing it forwards beating it on floor as it passes R. Take R shoulder backwards and bend R knee.
2. Place L firmly on floor.
3. Raise R swinging it forwards, beating it on floor as it passes L.

Bar 4.
1. Stamp R just in front of L, immediately transferring weight of body and stretching L behind.
2. Lift L heel *derrière*.
3. Pause.
   Repeat other foot.

   It is important to make an easy turn of the body from the waist upwards and make this contrast very clear when the opposite shoulder to leg is being used and when it is the same. The head must be kept upright, eyes directed forwards, only turning it to the audience with the stamp on R in the fourth bar.

6. Balancé.

Time signature 3/4. Commence normal position.

anacrusis. Stretch R *croisé devant* raising it slightly.

1. Step R *en place*, bending knee and raising L *demi-pointe* just behind R ankle, transferring weight of body and bending it slightly backwards.
2. Just take weight of body on L *demi-pointe* behind R.
3. Step R *fondu en place*, transferring weight and raising L toe pointed just behind R ankle.

Repeat commencing L foot.

This *balancé* is often followed by *pas de basque* commencing L foot (see No. 8). In this case the body would then bend sideways to left, R arm opening sideways before being raised *croisé en avant* with L hand on hip.

7.

This is a combination of *Balancé, pas de basque* and *pas de bourrée*.

Bars 1 and 2.

Balancé and *pas de basque* finishing L toe pointed and resting behind R ankle.

Bar 3.

1. Stamp L sharply making short step left, followed by quick hop L, raising R behind L, both legs turned-out.
2. Land on R *demi-pointe* as if coming in front of L.
3. Step L *éffacé fondu* in front of R, which is slightly bent.

Bar 4.

1. Step R into 4th *croisé devant* immediately transferring weight of body. Straighten R knee, L remaining *derrière*, but rising to *demi-pointe*. Body is now straight, head turned to right.

3 – 4. Pause.

This can be danced commencing L foot.

8. Pas de Basque.

There are several forms. The first is now only found in older ballets (Petipa, Gorsky etc): The second is in contemporary works.

First form.

Time signature 2/4. Commence normal or 3rd position.

1. Step forwards R *croisé fondu*, stretching L forwards just off floor and bring R shoulder forwards leaning body slightly backwards. Head is turned over R shoulder, R arm raised with elbow bent, hand just above head, L arm held sideways.
2. Step L immediately transferring weight and stretching R knee, begin to lower R arm to side.
3. Place R behind L simultaneously raising and stretching L *éffacé devant* as R sinks into *fondu*. Straighten body and turn it by bringing L shoulder forwards, raising L arm *éffacé devant* and above head.

Repeat commencing L foot.

9. Second form.

In this form the *pas de basque* resembles a *balancé*, but instead of placing the working foot behind the supporting leg on the second beat, it is placed in front. If the movement begins with the R foot, then on the first beat the R arm is opened to the side with a wide sweep and if desired then raised in front of the head. The L hand is usually held on the hip. The body usually turns with the R shoulder slightly forwards but head inclined to the left. During the second bar (beginning with the L foot) the R arm is circled down to the side, body and head turning to bring L shoulder forwards and head inclined to the left. The movement and direction of the feet do not change.

10. Third form. (Used by Fokine).

Time signature. 3/4. Commence 3rd position. R *devant*.

1. Slightly spring forwards on R, bringing L forwards lifted just off floor.
2. Small step forwards L *demi-pointe*.
3. Bring R foot to L and place it slightly in front.
   Repeat other foot.

The spring must be very slight and is somewhat similar to the *skid* of Polish and Hungarian dance, but is much lighter and a little higher.

11. Fourth form.
Time signature 2/4. Commence normal position.
anacrusis. Raise R, knee bent, toe resting on L ankle.
1. Slightly spring on R, immediately transferring weight and turning body to right, knee is slightly bent as L foot is brought in front of R ankle.
and. Step L *demi-pointe croisé devant* (i.e. small 4th).
2. Stamp R, bringing L to R ankle.
and. Pause.
   Repeat other foot.
   R arm is usually held in front and L behind body roughly at waist level, both elbows bent. Arms change position as step is repeated.

12. Glissade.
Time signature 3/4. Commence normal position. L hand with fingers straight on hip, R arm, elbow bent across chest, body straight but R shoulder is brought slightly forwards, head turned to left.
anacrusis. Bending R knee, raise foot behind L ankle (L *fondu*), slightly inclining body to right.
1. Step to right on R *fondu*, stretching L sideways to *pointe tendue* simultaneously opening R arm sideways to shoulder level, palm upwards. Body and head bend slightly towards L foot.
2. Glide L foot towards R, which begins to bend. Do not change position of body or head.
3. Step on L (it is roughly in small 4th *devant*), which immediately rises as on anacrusis above. Simultaneously bend R elbow.
   Repeat same foot.
   It is essential to use a good turn-out for this step.

13. Sissonne No. 1 with Pas de Bourrée.
This is very like a classical *sissonne ordinaire* but danced with a sharp clear accent.
Time signature 6/8. Commence R 3rd position R *devant*.
1. *Demi-plié* into *sissonne ouverte* to R *pointe tendue*.
2. Step R *demi-pointe* behind L.
3. Small step sideways to left on L, closing 3rd position *demi-plié*.
4. Stamp R into small 4th *devant*, transferring weight to R and resting L *demi-pointe* on floor.
5 – 6. Pause.

Repeat other side.

Arms are usually raised into 3rd with *sissonne*, R shoulder brought slightly forwards and head turned *écarté*. The arms then open sideways, but as feet close together R arm usually bends across front and L behind body, elbows bent just below chest level.

14. Sissonne No. 2 with Turn.

Time signature 6/8. Commence 3rd position.

anacrusis. Quick *demi-plié*, open arms sideways.

1. Slightly hop L, raising R foot behind L ankle and beginning to turn to right. Bring L shoulder forwards, L arm, elbow bent across chest, R behind waist. Turn head left (see sketch below and note there are three variations for this).
2. Step R *demi-pointe* behind L. (Dancer is now back to audience, L foot not raised from floor.) Straighten body bringing arms closer to each other by lowering one and raising the other.
3. Step L *demi-pointe* behind R, thus completing turn. Open arms sideways, L arm slightly higher than R.
4. Stamp R in small 4th. Both knees are slightly bent as body inclines forwards to right together with head and R shoulder. Change arms.
5 – 6. Pause.

The movement can now be repeated with same foot, in which case R leg should be lifted into low attitude on last beat. This *pas de bourrée* should always be danced *sur les demi-pointes*.

15. Pas de Bourrée Renversé.

This begins as No. 14 above, but on second beat do not straighten the body instead bend it backwards and to the left as far as possible whilst closing arms into 1st position at shoulder level. On third beat raise R leg higher, before opening R arm to side and placing L behind. Head is as before when stamping well forwards on fourth beat. On this beat curve R arm round upper body and L over head (see sketch above).

This step is usually only danced by girls.

16. Rond de jambe en l'air. No. 1.

This step is usually combined with *pas de bourrée* and occupies two bars, i.e. one for the *rond de jambe* and one for the *pas de bourrée*.
Time signature 3/4. Commence 4th *Croisé* L *pointe tendue derrière*.

Bar 1.
1. *Coupé* transferring weight of body (N.B. this movement must travel through whole foot from toe to firm tap of heel on floor) stretching R sideways to 25°.
2. Hop L simultaneously with *petit rond de jambe en l'air* R.
3. Return R to position of 25° and slightly bend L knee.

Bar 2.
1. Commence *pas de bourrée* stepping R behind L, and bringing L foot in front of R ankle.
2. Small step L to left on *demi-pointe* beside R, knee slightly bent and raising R arm as in *pas de bourrée*.

3. Stamp R in 4th *croisé devant* with *demi-plié,* transferring weight of body and raising L foot to level of R ankle.

In older ballets the classical form of *ports de bras* is used, i.e. during *rond de jambe* both arms circle from preparatory to 1st and up to 3rd position before opening to 2nd and during the *pas de bourrée* are held in preparatory position. In present day productions other *ports de bras* are used, e.g. during first bar raise R arm over head and place L hand on hip or out sideways, whilst bringing L shoulder slightly forwards as body inclines to left. Turn head to left with eyes glancing down. On second bar, R arm gradually opens to side before closing across in front and behind waist. On last beat bring R shoulder slightly forwards and turn head to right.

17. Rond de jambe. No. 2.

Another version of the *rond de jambe* is danced particularly by girls. It must be smooth and the body held very controlled. The circling of the leg is done

without a hop on the supporting one. R arm with elbow bent is held at the side as the R hand makes a small circle together with the *rond de jambe*.

This form is often used in an *enchainement* of 4 bars. First and second bars consist of the above *rond de jambe* and *pas de bourrée*. The third and fourth bars are a repeat of No. 1, which is danced almost *en place* and not forwards. The body is kept almost upright, turning only very slightly from side to side. The arms must not rise above chest level.

18. Pas de Chat.
The *pas de chat* is often used effectively to end an *enchainement* or variation. This resembles the *pas de basque sauté* of classical dance, but the movement must not travel far because the first circling movement and spring on to the leading foot to change weight, brings that foot into a small 2nd position and the following step is taken into a small 4th *croisé devant* on *demi-pointe*.

19. Pas de Chat and Walk.
This *pas de chat* can be combined with step No. 1 which is usually danced *en place*. In this case the arms, particularly those of the boys, are raised in 3rd during the *pas de chat* and circled down, one in front and the other behind the body during the turn.

20. Saut de Basque.
The boys also dance the *saut de basque* as in Hungary (see No. 27 in Hungarian Dance). Their arms move altogether more broadly with typical Spanish positions of the hand (see sketches p. 108–9).

21. Chassé and Stamp.
The basis for this *chassé* is the same as in any classical *chassé*. The dancer moves forwards or sideways smoothly, but in Spanish dance it must have greater precision and emphasis.
Time signature 3/4. Commence 3rd, R *devant*; L shoulder slightly forwards, L arm, elbow bent behind waist; R arm elbow bent and hand clenched above head and directed towards L shoulder.

anacrusis. Simultaneously *demi-plié* and bring R leg fully stretched to *éffacé devant*, just off floor.

1. Bring R foot back to L on *quarter pointe* transferring weight of body then stretch L to left then towards R and place it on *demi-pointe* beside R.
2. Lightly stamp R placing whole foot on floor moving very slightly left and bending knee as body begins to turn left bend L knee and raise foot from floor. Lower R arm in front of face as L arm comes forwards.
3. Stamp L foot in 3rd *devant* and immediately stretch it outwards into 4th *éffacé* just off floor, R foot must not move. Bring R shoulder forwards and fold R arm behind waist lifting L above head.

Repeat step to L.

22. Dropping to the knee.

In Spanish dance boys and girls often kneel. In the majority of cases it is the boy dropping to his knees in homage to the girl. He rises on *demi-pointes* and falls on both knees, body curved slightly backwards, both arms rounded and held downwards behind the body.

The girl on the other hand springs on to one foot before dropping on to the other knee and can thus kneel with the body curved only slightly backwards. The head also inclines or turns that way with one arm curved across the chest the other over her head. Or she can sink further to the floor bending her body further backwards by raising one arm over her head and the other stretch backwards. The sketch below shows how the pose can be *croisé* or *éffacé*.

CHARACTER DANCE

23. Pas de Bourrée.
As used in Gorsky's production of *Swan Lake* is also widely used, particularly when working for neat quick beats.
Time signature 3/4. Commence R foot held on L ankle.

Bar 1.
1. Place R *demi-pointe* in small 4th *devant* taking weight of body and bring shoulder R forwards and just raising L foot before placing it on *demi-pointe* behind R, immediately tap R *demi-pointe* beside L, which rises to level of R ankle. (N.B. All three movements on first beat. All on *demi-pointes* and knees not fully stretched.)
2. Repeat above commencing L foot.
3. Place L heel on floor transferring weight and tap R *demi-pointe* in 3rd *devant* without dropping heel or bending knee, then immediately stretch R leg *éffacé devant*.

Bar 2.
1. Return R to 3rd position, again raise *éffacé* and return to 3rd but drop heel and *demi-plié*, transferring weight whilst raising L foot behind R ankle.
2. Tap L *demi-pointe* behind R, raising R then placing it beside L without lowering heel. (N.B. two movements on each of these 2 beats.)
3. Stamp L in 3rd, transferring weight fully and raising R behind L ankle as before.

If this sequence of *pas de bourrée* and *battements tendus* is to be repeated with other foot, then on last beat of second bar the dancer must make a clear *coupé* to change feet.

24. Stepping on *Demi-pointes* (as in Loupoukov's Don Quixote).
Time signature 3/4. Commence normal position, arms folded behind body, wrists crossed at waist level.

Bar 1.
1. Step forwards R *demi-pointe*, L also rests on *demi-pointe*. Bring R shoulder forwards a little higher than L shoulder, body slightly inclined backwards to left.
2. With a sharp tap bring L behind R to 3rd *derrière* on *demi-pointe*. Knees all but fully stretched.

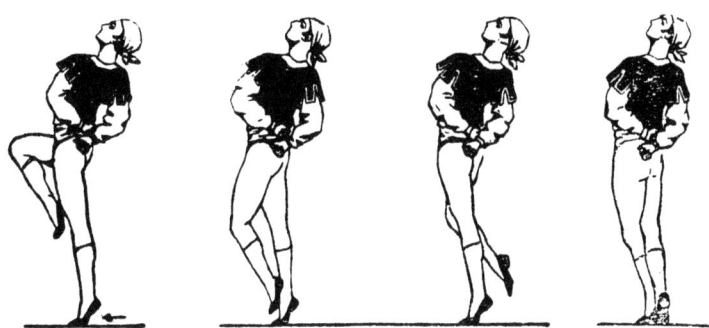

3. Spring slightly upwards bending both knees and complete jump in 3rd on *demi-pointes*, increasing depth of *demi-plié*.

Bar 2.
1. Raise R knee bent *(tirebouchon) devant* whilst stepping forwards on L *demi-pointe* and stretching L knee, simultaneously bring L shoulder forwards with head turned and inclined slightly backwards.
2. Place R *demi-pointe* behind L immediately and slightly raising L foot and turning L shoulder to right before place L *demi-pointe* in front of R, which just rises from floor.
3. Stamp R behind L so that feet finish in 3rd position *demi-pointes*.

The whole of this movement must be danced on *demi-pointes* in spite of the clearly marked stamps on the floor. It is also essential to use the body correctly by bringing the opposite shoulder forwards to raised leg on the first beat of the second bar. The step should always be danced in profile to the audience and with the knees directed forwards.

25. Jump from the Basque countries frequently used on stage.
Time signature 2/4. Commence in easy 4th L *devant*.
anacrusis. Spring upwards from both feet and change their position in the air.
1. Land in large 4th *demi-pointes*.
2. Hold.

The important aspect of this jump is to maintain the level of the shoulders, particularly if repeating the movement, and then smoothly change the arms from one side to the other using the law of opposition.

www.ingramcontent.com/pod-product-compliance
Ingram Content Group UK Ltd.
Pitfield, Milton Keynes, MK11 3LW, UK
UKHW021321180426
11947UKWH00015B/1362